# THE RETURN TO SELF-CONCERN

# THE RETURN TO SELF-CONCERN

by

ALLEN F. BRAY, III

THE WESTMINSTER PRESS
Philadelphia

LIBRARY OF CONGRESS CATALOG CARD NO. 64-10517

PRINTED IN THE UNITED STATES OF AMERICA

PUBLISHED BY THE WESTMINSTER PRESS
Philadelphia, Pennsylvania 19107

*For*

LOUISE WHITEFIELD BRAY

1889–1963

*who in dying, lives;*

*and in knowing, rejoices.*

# CONTENTS

## *Acknowledgments*

"Of making many books there is no end," said the Preacher (Eccl. 12:12), but this is more significantly true in the case of acknowledgments. One's first book is the labor of many hands and the love of many hearts. Teachers, of course, are the great catalysts, and to me has been given the privilege of Howe, Zabriskie, Mollegen, Wedel, Stinnette, and Bowie, to mention but a few. In particular, my debt to Kendig Brubaker Cully for direction, patience, and enthusiasm is beyond expression.

There are as well, however, the known and unknown saints, scholars and faithful servants of the past and the present to whom I am deeply indebted. My especial thanks are due colleagues, students, parishioners, a host of friends, encouraging parents, and a generous wife and children, who gave that this might grow.

To and for all these, I give thanks. But for them, it would never have been, and such good as there is in it is ours rather than mine.

A. F. B.

*Culver Military Academy*
*Culver, Indiana*

# INTRODUCTION

The many names by which the modern age defines itself serve as well to indicate significant areas of strength and weakness. One of the more familiar of the designations is that this is " The Age of Conformity." The implication is not complimentary and it is not intended to be. Ours is the time and the culture in which the avowed concern for the individual is at perhaps the highest point since the Renaissance, yet in practice the concept and consequences of individuality are subordinated to the pressures and directions of " the group." There is, then, a disparity between our preaching and our practice, and the resulting confusion is of particular significance for the Christian church, which holds a primary trust and responsibility for the nurture of the individual.

The gulf between the profession and the practice of concern for the individual on the part of society points up the absence or neglect of the religious dimension in life without which the ideal of community becomes merely the practice of conformity. In the contemporary pattern there is not so much a trend toward rejection of the ideal as there is a trend to shallow and convenient acceptance of it. The rich and full meaning of individuality has not been recognized or acknowledged because we have been too busy proclaiming our allegiance to the principle to fully comprehend it or actually commit ourselves to it. The failure, then, lies not so much in the principle as in the prostitution of it, as suggested by Erich Fromm:

> The failure of modern culture lies not in its principle of individualism, of self-interest, but in the deterioration of the meaning of self-interest; not in the fact that people are too much concerned with their self-interest, but that they are not concerned enough with the interest of their real self; not in the fact that they are too selfish, but that they do not love themselves.[1]

This indictment presents clearly the paradox that if the individual is to be community-centered or community-concerned in the healthful sense of such terms, there must be, as a primary and constant factor, self-awareness and self-interest. Apart from or in the absence of the knowledge of himself, the individual can neither contribute to nor participate in either the context or the contest of community. The paradoxical demands of individuality in community are so vaguely defined that the individual fears they can never be realized or have their tensions resolved. The variety of pressures under which he or she operates are so many and so strong that the individual cannot help questioning the possible existence of a single unifying purpose in the strength of which there can be labor and out of the bond of which there can grow love.

The world in which the individual of today finds himself is nearly as confusing as the quality of life he believes himself called upon to live. Demands from within the self are challenged and countered by demands from without. The pressure of the secular culture is such that, given the opportunity for decision, the individual almost instinctively tends to be disloyal to his self and chooses the pattern of the group of which he counts himself — or hopes to become — a part. The need to belong is so strong that little thought is given as to who is belonging to what. Like the hurly-burly of the carnival, modern life offers something for everyone, young and old, fat or thin, tall or short. The voice of the huckster subjects every age, every group, every class, to pleas and pressures. Sometimes the voice is smooth and seductive and sometimes it is strong and crass, but almost never is it quiet.

To discover in the midst of this plethora of demands and designs a comprehensive and consistent sense of purpose suitable for both aspiration and adoption requires recognition and cognizance of the basic entity, the self. Whatever the culture or the crowd, whatever the age or the aegis, " maintenance of the real self is of primary significance for the individual. It is the most stable consistent value in his life." [2] In the search for purpose, then, for lasting meaning in his life, the individual must begin with and within himself.

The search for selfhood is not an easy one, nor is it lightly undertaken. There is, on the one hand, the problem of recognition. Who am I? The self is not static. To the contrary, it is dynamic, in a constant state of growth and change. This dynamism has both positive and negative manifestations, but it is never at rest. There is, on the other hand, the problem of responsibility. Did I do that? Should I do that? The responsibility of individuality cannot be resisted or refused any more than the other implications of selfhood. It acts as a spotlight, singling the individual out from all the contemporaries.

The search for selfhood is further complicated by the problem of motive. Modern man has been conditioned to work for a cause. He will sacrifice for and contribute time, talent, and money to a variety of drives. In the interest of the crippled, the tubercular, the fatherless, the unwed, the new church, the village memorial, etc., almost any means is justified by the end. But is the search for and discovery of the self a valid cause? Is not this the epitome of selfishness? Is it not the better part to subordinate individual desires and aspirations into the acceptable patterns of mass behavior? The question confounding modern man is, in brief: Is it legitimate (morally speaking) and acceptable (culturally speaking) to be self-concerned? In his nobler moments, modern man loves his neighbor because he would like to be loved himself. But he fears to love himself in order that he may love his neighbor!

Perhaps the most immediate and dangerous consequence of the search for selfhood is the removal of the protective shell of society from around the individual. Man's dilemma is that he must acquaint himself with his self, he must admit himself to his self, and this process requires separation and distinction from others. Unless and until he discovers himself as an individual, however, the society of which he is at least a token part will be the less. The fearful corollary to this is that the less society receives from the individual, the less it can contribute to him. Any human society is, in the final analysis, but the sum total of the individuals who comprise it, their combined joys and weaknesses, strengths and fears. Thus the concern for and concept of selfhood is of vital importance to each person and to all persons. It may be defined as " the consciousness of one's personality as distinct from others, and as the reality of this awareness in the individual's being able to assert his distinction." [3]

Herein, then, lies the basic paradox of the search for selfhood: to be a contributing member of society requires the acceptance of the responsibility of individuality. But this brings with it the threat of separation. This threat is often more powerful as a motivating force than the promise of the actual community wherein a sense of responsible selfhood is accepted and acknowledged. At the moment of decision the individual is torn between the light comfort of such protection as he may find in conformity and the consequences of responsible individuality, the essential ingredient of genuine community. Individuality in the sense of self-integrity stands in opposition to conformity for the sake of actual community.

The individual does not, however, face his moment of truth alone or unarmed. He is, in fact, surrounded by a host of victorious witnesses and has available to him strong resources for the conduct and successful conclusion of the search. Both religion and psychiatry are aware of the tendency on the part of the individual to neglect his self and to settle for the seemingly acceptable substitute of conformity in place of community. Both assert, however, that only as confusions are clarified and misunderstandings resolved is there the possibility that the individual personality will be able to respond to the demands and challenges of his time, using the illumination of the past and walking toward the promise of the future.

As perhaps never before, the individual of today needs an illumination and interpretation of his present from beyond the existential moment and yet relevant to it. He believes and seeks help for his unbelief. His desire is not to relinquish but to redeem the world in which he finds himself. Thus religion should and must be a vital part of his searching activity and the resources thereof. Apart from religious insight and awareness, the individual will have an inadequate and imperfect self-portrait. Divorced from or oblivious of the religious factor, man's life is minus a vital dimension.

By virtue of its educational and pastoral commission, the Christian church must speak clearly to and walk comfortingly with the individual in his search for selfhood. The primary work of the church if it is true to the pattern of its Lord is the work of reconciliation. This involves not only the meeting between God and man and man and man, but perhaps most significantly the meeting between man and himself. Christian education, then, by both its commission and its expressed concern is confronted with the responsibility to communicate and enable the individual to comprehend the total dimension of his life. Because the peril of humanistic sophistry continues to walk abroad, the Christian church must speak its truth strongly, clearly, and relevantly. The words of Paul to the sophisticated but shallow who were gathered on Mars' Hill could well be adopted as the statement of purpose: "I perceive that in all things ye are too superstitious. For as I passed by, and beheld your devotions, I found an altar with this inscription, TO THE UNKNOWN GOD. Whom therefore ye ignorantly worship, him declare I unto you" (Acts 17:22-23).

If the church is to speak to modern man, it must recognize the full spectrum of factors that influence him. It must take into account not only the technological advances that have become so prominent within the last half century but the psychological consequences of a technologically centered civilization. Furthermore, it must acknowledge and accept advancements in other fields perhaps less obvious but no less important. The responsibility for wholeness that is a concomitant of the search for selfhood places a weighty burden upon the individual in our time, and he stands in great need of the reconciling word of a religious faith that is comprehensive enough to be relevant to his confusion and his striving, and faithful enough to present a perspective that is not limited to the " principalities and powers " of this world.

> Since we cannot and will not turn our backs on the modern world, then the religion we embrace cannot be pre-scientific; nor anti-scientific; it must be co-scientific. But science alone produces none of the integrity, the direction, or the zeal, that are needed in order to assure the benefits of its own achievements. It is up to modern man, the weaver, to take the strands of science and bind them with values and purpose. No threads may be rejected, perhaps least of all those that come from modern psychology, psychiatry, and psychoanalysis. For to apply the prophetic teachings of past ages to a technical age requires special assistance from the sciences that deal with personality and with human relations.[4]

Reinhold Niebuhr once pointed out that there is no greater futility than the answer to a question no one has asked. To avert this, Christian education is assisted in learning the questions that are asked through the cooperative insights of its ally, psychiatry. Not only the insights but the methodologies of this vital field have been developed out of man's sometimes tortured but always sincere portrayal in depth of his situation as he experiences and attempts to understand and control it.

Although the perspective of psychiatry and its definition of the goal may differ from that of the Christian faith, these are not necessarily barriers to cooperation, nor do they deny the possible strength of mutual concern. The immediate nature of the concern of the medical therapist does contrast with the ultimate nature of the concern represented by the religious counselor, but both share in a common method, therapy, or care.[5]

The individual in search of selfhood must also, however,

be prepared to face resistance in the course of his pilgrimage. One of the prime areas of such resistance is the relationship between the church and the culture. There is evident an increasing concern that the Christian church, despite its statistics, is less effective in the present day because it has fallen prey to conformity rather than given birth to community. Instead of being the leaven in the lump, the contemporary church has veered dangerously toward becoming a creature of the culture. To recover both its sense of mission and its effectiveness in that task, the contemporary church must do two things primarily: it must return and subject itself to the pattern and presence of its Lord, and it must listen with hearing ears to the voices of its sheep, to the cries of " they that be sick."

" The time has come when a re-examination of Christian education in the church is imperative. Such a re-examination should on the one hand consider the needs of our day which Christian education must meet and on the other hand evaluate the program as it is now being practiced." [6] The lessons of the past are available for the benefit of the present, and many are the voices in the present that are clear and strident in their demand for the fruit of past experience. Modern man is eager to respond to that which speaks truly and strongly to and of his real self. This applies to every generation and every level of society provided the communication is clear and the confrontation is relevant. The depth of the encounter may vary according to the age, condition, or experience of the individual, but for every person there are providential moments for communication, comprehension, and commitment. In the final analysis it is this individual encounter and the invitation from *beyond* life *for* life that releases the individual from the captivity of his culture and the restriction of his own finite creativity.

The lessons of history are often learned by parallelism. By way of illustration, there is a significant parallel between the first century of our era and the present day. As " the law " was to the first-century Jew, so has " science " become for many a twentieth-century sophisticate. "As at the beginning of the Christian Era, so again today we are faced with the problem of the moral backwardness which has failed to keep pace with our scientific, technical, and social developments." [7] Modern man, if not overcome by his technology, certainly appears to stand in dumbfounded awe of its potentialities and not a little in fear of its consequences.

The timidity and uncertainty of modern man in comparison with the boldness and strength of his scientific advances has been strikingly described by Carl Jung:

> We all say that this is the century of the common man, that he is the lord of the earth, the air and the water, and that on his decision hangs the historical fate of the nations. This proud picture of human grandeur is unfortunately an illusion only and is counter-balanced by a reality which is very different. In this reality man is the slave and victim of the machines that have conquered space and time for him; he is intimidated and endangered by the might of the war technique which is supposed to safeguard his physical existence; his spiritual and moral freedom, though guaranteed within limits in one half of his world, is threatened with chaotic disorientation, and in the other half it is abolished altogether. Finally, to add comedy to tragedy, this lord of the elements, this universal arbiter, hugs to his bosom notions which stamp his dignity as worthless and turn his autonomy into an absurdity.[8]

What follows is an attempt to recover a consciousness of pattern and purpose on the part of the Christian church in general and Christian education in particular to the intent that a more singular and effective voice may speak to and with the children of this age out of the relevant context of eternal truth. Aided and informed by the resources of both this world and the next, Christian education is empowered so to minister to the individual that he may discover and be deepened in his consciousness of the gift of selfhood to the benefit of himself and his society and to the glory of God. As it is willing not only to recognize but to enter into the arena of alienation and lead therefrom the anxious child of this age, Christian education in particular and the Christian church in general exercises its vital task and trust of nurture both relevantly and faithfully.

The thesis of the following pages is twofold: that the struggle which modern man experiences as a member of society and the consequent anxiety that dogs his steps is but a reflection of the struggle and the anxiety within himself; and that such a philosophy of pastoral care, of nurture and education as is herein proposed, is not new, but a reemergence of the purpose and philosophy once seen in Him who " taught them as one having authority, and not as the scribes " (Matt. 7:29) . It suggests and signifies a return to self-concern.

# I

# THE CONTEMPORARY SCENE

*Behold, your house is left unto you desolate: and verily I say unto you, Ye shall not see me, until the time come when ye shall say, Blessed is he that cometh in the name of the Lord.*

— Luke 13:35.

# *Chapter One*

# MODERN MAN: HIS SITUATION

Perhaps the most striking thing about modern man is his apparently boundless activity. His is a life spent constantly on the move emotionally if not geographically. The rapidity of both his action and his thought outdistances even the miracle of modern transportation. Twentieth-century living may be more aptly characterized by its pace than its purpose, and the contemporary individual is the victim of both the speed and the practice. The activities in which modern man is involved and the rate at which he proceeds from one to the other reflect not so much his capability as they do the pressure under which he lives. A vast complex of demands, both external and internal, organizes and directs the life of twentieth-century man.

The child of this age, however, appears to be subject to the pressure of external more than internal forces. A strong desire for cultural acceptance and favor dictates that he reflect in his appearance, his thinking, and his speaking, the credos of his time and his society. This is the nucleus of the conformity that is popularly defined as "crowd culture." It makes of man an object rather than a subject, an item rather than an entity.[1]

This pressure which is exerted upon the individual from outside is matched by the pressure that he exerts upon himself — the pressure from within. This represents the greater tension, for within himself the individual wages the fiercest war between conformity and self-integrity. No person easily or willingly relinquishes his subjectivity. His resistance to external pressures, to the demands to subscribe to the norm, to conform, is colored however faintly by an innate sense of personal integrity and individual worth. One of the prime pitfalls of modern man is the challenge to " Keep up! " Before he is conscious of his participation he is registered and running, so completely involved that he has little if any time or opportunity to ask why he must keep up, or with what. The infrequent moment he has for himself leaves even less for others. The pace and fullness of contemporary life breeds separation and restriction.

In order to preserve his sanity — or some semblance of purpose to his life — modern man attempts to compartmentalize his activities and his interests. This might well be called the age of the appointment book, and it is provided for both home and office. Catastrophic indeed is the occasion when they are out of synchronization! The plethora of responsibilities, both social and professional, faced by the young couple attempting to " Keep up! " is staggering and cannot help resulting in fragmentation. So conscious of the separate pieces of his life as portrayed by hours and dates on lined and numbered pages, the individual loses sight of the totality, the comprehensive unity, of his life. There appears to be no forest, only trees. The result is frustration and failure rather than purposeful comprehension and unification of the related aspects. The tragedy lies in " the fact that what he has palmed off as an enrichment is really an impoverishment, a simple lack of integrity. Instead of saying, ' I don't know what to make of myself ' jestingly, he would have to recognize the grim implications of that statement." [2]

Much of what we count as normal activity is pursued for purposes that are, at best, vague and ill-defined. The energy this pursuit calls forth from the individual leaves him too depleted to evaluate either the cause or the end of his effort. Locked in the solitary confinement of his own undefined concern, he is separated from his fellows, although they may be as close as the other end of the dining table. Such barriers within families, within business firms, within social fellowships, testify to an increasingly dangerous lack of basic communication. Perhaps not so strange as it seems is that fact that " this separateness exists in the very places where the greatest numbers of people are herded together, as in the cities." [3]

The situation in which modern man finds himself can be expressed in many ways. Perhaps the most appropriate, at least for the nurturing responsibility of the Christian church, is man's self-expression, his " profile " as it were, drawn from the self-revelation contained in his productivity, some of his art forms, his religion, and his politics. These may well be the most accurate analyses of what man feels and thinks about himself and his purpose, not to mention his goal. Singly and in combination, these facets serve as something of an autobiography. Neither the scope nor the space of this work allows for anything approaching exhaustive analyses of these areas, and other persons far more competent have made such studies available; therefore, what follows is a sketch rather than a detailed portrait of man as he defines himself in this age.

The Gross National Product is something in which every individual who is aware of it, whether or not he comprehends the fullness of the term, takes great pride. That child of the Industrial Revolution, the Machine Age, may have its contributions viewed in many lights, but subsequent history will undoubtedly devote much attention to its major by-product — leisure. The invention and easy availability of the so-called labor-saving devices have posed not only a paradise but a challenge for the individual. The marvel of automation has brought with it the curse of uselessness or sloth, depending on which side of the bargaining table you sit. Serious efforts toward the retraining of workers are challenged by demands — increasingly successful — for a thirty-five-hour workweek at a sixty-hour wage rate.

Time hangs heavy on the hands of many a modern, yet he

counts it as of the essence and places a higher priority on quantity than on quality. One cannot say, as in other times, that ease and comfort are the prime desirables. Pleasure and plenty are the shining goals for many in this time. There is indeed a disturbing indication of devotion to the symbols rather than the realities of growth. Submission to this unfortunate tendency causes the individual to experience " the consequent loss of the dimension of depth in his encounter with reality." [4] Thus there is a confusion which fosters chaos in the quality of our living and our striving.

One of the most outstanding psychological features of modern life is the fact that activities which are means to ends have more and more usurped the position of ends, while the ends themselves have a shadowy and unreal existence. People work in order to make money; they make money in order to do enjoyable things with it. The work is the means, the enjoyment, the end. But what happens actually? People work in order to make more money; they use this money to make still more money, and the end – the enjoyment of life – is lost sight of. People are in a hurry and invent things in order to have more time. Then they use the time saved to rush about again to save more time until they are so exhausted that they cannot use the time they saved.[5]

The confusion and/or distortion of values and views held by the contemporary individual is revealed not only by the nature and purpose of his mechanical productivity. A similar pattern may be observed in his art forms, notably contemporary theater and literature. In the period since the close of World War II much of the legitimate stage has been concerned with a rather morose portrayal of the decadent consequences of man alone in a world of his own creation — a world in which man has lost his footing and which daily threatens to devour him in his entirety. The paranoidal dreams of a Willy Loman are shared by many who could not thus give them voice. The tragic fantasy of a Blanche Du Bois is but the highlighting of the compromise that seduces many a lost child of this time.

There are several dominant strains in the contemporary

theater which are distinguishable. There is the school of stark realism which ranges from the chronicle of Anne Frank to the tortured catharsis of an O'Neill or a Williams. The interpretive portrayals of an Inge or a Miller present a subjective sensitivity to tragedy with which identification is all too easy. The avant-garde attempts of the "off-Broadway" circuit, with its dedication to the pseudoexistentialist dramas, represents a half-brave attempt to recognize the nature of modern man and a half-cowardly attempt to accept rather than resolve the dilemma. The pleasant and whimsical fantasies of a Meredith or Lerner and Loewe provide release from concern and contention by removal to "fantasyland." Each of these trends, however, reveals a sense of dissatisfaction with what is now, a strong tide of discontent with "the way things are," and a desire to escape.

Similar patterns are to be found in contemporary literature. On the basis of both quality and content, one might say there appears to be a concern to depict as graphically as possible the erotically stimulating but emotionally frustrating and spiritually deadening aspects of a world and a time in which irresponsible man is freed of all accountability for his actions and, consequently, has no recourse for redemption. In point of fact, the quality of such contemporary writing reflects the weakness and shallowness of modern man far better than the technical portrayals contained therein.

Much of modern writing reflects the immediacy of man's concern for himself and his world. It serves to illustrate the powerfulness of the principle of expediency and the extent to which men will go in an effort either to escape (as in the case of alcoholic or narcotic addiction) or to succumb (as in the case of homosexuality or heterosexual promiscuity). Throughout this contemporary writing, there runs the single thread of a haunting dissatisfaction with what is portrayed, and an undefined desire for the knowledge and strength that is both essential and appropriate to man if he is to become what he would like and is called to be.

Modern man also defines himself in the light and in terms

of his philosophy. Although this might be considered as a positive factor, Carl Jung asserts that it represents in actuality nothing more than an emasculated rationalism. " Our philosophy is no longer a way of life, as it was in antiquity; it has turned into an exclusively intellectual and academic affair." [6]

There is, for example, the school of atheistic existentialism whose high priest is Jean-Paul Sartre. As a philosophy, existentialism is of an earlier time, but the shortsighted desperation of atheistic existentialism is peculiarly a phenomenon of the twentieth century. It represents man's attempt to rise above his situation by condemning it; yet it reveals his unwillingness or inability to evaluate the standard by which this judgment is made. Paul Tillich suggests that this represents a protest against industrial society from within, and this may well be the case.[7]

The mood of Sartre, Camus, and others of the popular school is that of a qualified despair informed, in the main, by a weak self-pity. The paradox is that a philosophy of the inadequate and unsatisfactory present is at the same time a reflection of a contributing past and a promise of a future. No judgment is completely isolated; it is informed by a sense of what has gone before and the expectation, be it hopeful or fearful, of what may come after. As in the classic example, Sartre's *No Exit,* the inconsistency lies in the fact that such a portrayal of limitation, of finitude, is possible only within a context of freedom and the possibility of infinity.

A derivative form of atheistic existentialism is peculiar to the American scene and to the last decade. This is the movement whose members are customarily referred to as the Beat Generation. Strongly condemnatory of the conformity demanded by the culture, this movement establishes as an alternative a more insidious form of conformity known as nonconformity. The Beats assert that they are in revolt. They do not define, however, save in the vague jargon that is proof of their membership, either the focus of their effort or the nature of their proposed reconstruction of society.

Perhaps more than any other, this movement is indicative of the chaos of contemporary American culture. It is, in essence, a resistance movement — resistance to the denial of the privilege and the opportunity for the expression of individuality. If the search for selfhood is the purpose and cultural denial the opportunity of the cause, the goal will not be achieved merely by resistance to or reaction against the established pattern. There must be an alternative, and not a new authoritarianism but a truer freedom is the lasting dynamic and hope of the endeavor. Camus himself reminds us of the danger of superficial concern when he writes: "A society founded on signs is, in its essence, an artificial society in which man's carnal truth is handled as something artificial." [8]

Modern man gives yet another definition of himself in the conduct and concern expressed in his religious activity. In many areas and in many ways, contemporary religion not only has given way to but has taken on the cultural "image." The disappointment and dissatisfaction with this is being increasingly expressed in a variety of ways. One lay member of a church expressed her reaction in these words: "The parochial Mickey Mouse doesn't inspire us as being worth the sacrifice of time from business or professional life. At worst, the bazaars, committee meetings, Church school bedlams, suppers and fun nights, are abominations unto the Lord. At best they are merely irrelevant." [9]

Elton Trueblood makes the point that "the major danger of our contemporary religion . . . is that it makes small what ought to be large." [10] In its desire to be agreeable and thereby acceptable, contemporary religion has been guided by the egocentric demands of man more than by the theocentric declaration of eternal purpose. It is small wonder that we experience a confusion as to direction and a blurring of meaning.

With the erosion of particularity and the blurring of the line between church and world, the "People of God" has come to be a relatively meaningless conception. Everyone "belongs" with minimal commitment at minimal expense. Success-minded congregations make it all too clear in their solicitation that admission to the church is by handshake with the smiling pastor. The church that opens its door so easily loses its potency to evoke authentic personhood out of community. Few are asked to take the form of a servant, but all are frequently asked to take a packet of envelopes for financial contributions. No one is religious because everyone is "religious." [11]

All too seldom is the clarion call of Christian truth for action heard in our land in our time. "Contemporary preaching rarely goes further than to condemn men for sins against society; rare indeed is the sermon that condemns sin against a holy God." [12] In the minds of many, the local church is a place to *get* rather than a place to sacrificially *give* something, and the delusion has grown from within. The parish leaflet is rich with the trivia and the superficialities that have been conveniently substituted for the fundamentals of the faith. The consequence is that the individual in search of that which will sustain his selfhood finds no bold fellowship of the committed, but "a complacent society concerned to an absurd degree with its own internal politics. . . . Many contemporary seekers cannot abide the Church as they see it, their dissatisfaction arising not from the fact that membership demands too much, but rather from the fact that the demands are too small." [13]

The diet offered by the contemporary church in the majority of instances is a full one, but it is much like the modern miracle, cellulose, which has no taste, no smell, no residue, no effect, and gives only temporary satisfaction from the pangs of hunger. The anxious pagan, the distraught humanist, confronting the American church, finds in too many communities not strength but substitutes, not holiness but hollowness. The building of new churches, the enlargement and redecoration of existing structures, are heralded as signs of concern and growth. The evidence of architecture, however, is not always corroborated by the evident practice of personal discipleship. Buildings and calendars may illustrate a depth of devotion and devout range of activities, but they also may not do so. What actually takes place in the lives of individuals is of far greater moment than the seating capacity of or the bookings for the parish hall. The question posed by Paul Elmen is realistic and deserving of an answer: " Is not a man in trouble if he comes to the community church looking for the strong-crusted bread of God, and is given for his spiritual nourishment a church supper? Is he very likely to hear the sound of the great wings at a meeting of the men's club, when the warden of the local penitentiary speaks on revisions in the penal code? " [14]

Modern man has seen the instruments for his peace become the devices for his peril. The contributions of technical, cultural, and philosophical as well as religious developments have been so contained and molded by the culture that they have obscured rather than revealed, and confused rather than converted. It is no wonder that the individual has succumbed to the pressure, accepted the convenience of conformity, and established only such goals for his living and his aspiring as have the cultural seal of approval. Nature, we are told, abhors a vacuum. Man is a natural creature, and it ought to be of little wonder that into the void created by the abdication of the contemporary church from its pastoral responsibility there has come a new religion in an old skin — idolatry.

We forget that the essence of idolatry is not the worship of this or that particular idol but is a specifically human attitude. This attitude may be described as the deification of things, of partial aspects of the world and man's submission to such things, in contrast to an attitude in which his life is devoted to the realization of the highest principles of life, those of love and reason, to the aim of becoming what he potentially is, a being made in the likeness of God. It is not only pictures in stone and wood that are idols. Words can become idols, and machines can become idols; leaders, the state, power, and political groups may also serve. Science and the opinion of one's neighbors can become idols, and God has become an idol for many.[15]

## *Chapter Two*

# THE SEARCH AND THE SOLUTION

Modern man is neither pleased nor satisfied with the self-portrait he discerns in his productivity, his drama and literature, his philosophy or his religion. He is disturbed not only by what he recognizes as all too true there, but by the bubbling undercurrents of his selfhood seeking genuine expression for its reality. The latest in home improvements, the newest in residential communities, the most in creature comforts, the greatest effort for the worthiest of humanitarian causes, fail to ease his concern. He continues to seek for something that is beneath and yet beyond all of this, something that will give lasting meaning to these manifestations and significant purpose to him. Goaded by his uneasiness, he is continually spurred on to further accomplishments and acquisitions, none of which brings peace and each of which brings with it new challenges and a further reminder of his continuing failure.

Neither physical improvements nor comfort, not worldly position or temporal security, brings to the individual the full measure of relief he needs and for which he seeks. Ease of life and avoidance of difficulties and dangers bring no surcease from the struggle within himself. If he is fortunate, he discovers before he has lived too long that he has been tilting at windmills, that he has mistaken the enemy. He learns that satisfaction comes not always from the averting of the trials and tribulations of human life but from the meeting and overcoming of them. He discovers that these are, in fact, an essential ingredient in the responsible living of life as prophesied by Jesus of Nazareth: " In the world you have tribulation; but be of good cheer, I have overcome the world " (John 16:33). The meaning of the latter half of the quotation may not be as comforting to him as the first half is relevant, but he does realize that the enemy is not always outside, that sometimes he is within. Man's battle must first be won within himself if he would pursue his course in this world in spiritual peace and with strong purpose. Not the removal of difficulty, but the inward strength to accept and overcome it becomes the hope and desire of the troubled individual. A priority of purpose is thus established. This does not deny the reality of external conflict, of the often strong opposition of the natural order and the will of other individuals. It simply means, in the words of Stephen Neill, that " if man is to live as man should live, he needs to be reconciled to his environment and to his neighbours. But first and foremost he needs to be reconciled to himself." [1]

Because of the variety and strengths of the demands that are placed upon him by both society and himself, modern man appears unable to take the necessary time to recognize and accept himself for what he is, with a sound awareness of his twin capacities — for success and for failure. He is so busy doing that that he has no time for listening, and hardly any for an occasional moment of introspection, for self-evaluation. He is, in truth, " like a man who observes his natural face in a mirror; for he observes himself and goes away and at once forgets what he was like " (James 1:23-24). The rare glimpse that modern man has of his actual self is soon forgotten in the pressure of fitting the pattern that society prescribes if he is " to make something of himself."

In many ways the citizen of the twentieth century, particularly in Western democracy, tends to be the victim of a distortion of the " American dream." He has exchanged a sense of purpose for a zeal for possessions. He has traded his potentiality as a free and responsible self for a pottage of false pride in temporal ownership. Unable to visualize realistically a more significant goal, modern man strives to find and define himself in terms of his worldly goods. This philosophy of full barns bolsters his ego but defeats his desire for self-fulfillment, for "every attempt to seize freedom and to realize the self from man's side reflects not freedom but the bondage of self-idolatry."[2] By such a false solution and all akin to it, man is encouraged in his frustration by the various agencies of a culture whose concern increasingly turns upon immediate and material possessions rather than long-range purpose. The deliberate and insidious campaigns of such agencies are clearly revealed by exposures similar to that of Vance Packard's *The Hidden Persuaders.*[3] The nature of the loneliness and the extent of the desperation of the modern individual for some semblance of lasting meaning is to be seen in his enthusiastically naïve acceptance of substitutes.

Such loneliness, however, is not of the nature or to the benefit of man. Deep within himself he senses this. Thus it is that regardless of the effort of his striving or the measure of his success, he remains discontent and uneasy. The sensation as experienced defies definition, but is manifested in a general malaise, a diffuse dissatisfaction with "the way things are." Modern man has been with some accuracy typified by an apprehensiveness bordering on fear, which he can attribute to no apparent cause or lay to any specific concern. The generality of this malaise is signified by the description of this period as the Age of Anxiety. The full meaning of the phrase and its appropriateness for the contemporary individual has been well enunciated by Wayne Oates:

> Man fretfully grasps at the uncertain security of the temporal. When man, as in the case of economic anxiety, sets his heart upon the security of the temporal, succeeds in grasping it, and depends upon it for his ultimate satisfaction, this very satisfaction itself turns to ashes. . . . Economic anxiety is the conscious expression of a deeper and more diffuse kind of anxiety over the shortness of life, the set end of man's days.[4]

To find and know himself as he actually is, the individual requires a frame of reference in which he can be understood and out of which he can understand. It must be personal in its dynamic if he is to appreciate it and find appreciation for his self. The disinterestedness of contemporary society is such that man faces by himself and out of context enemies of whose existence he is not certain and whose characteristics are not clearly definable. They elude both his recognition and his definition. He faces them, for the most part, without resources. They are ghostly foes, and the riches and material resources of this world cannot prevail against them. His anxiety is fundamentally an anxiety of purpose — or the lack of it. Negatively, it has been defined by Paul Tillich as the anxiety of meaninglessness: " the loss of an ultimate concern, of a meaning which gives meaning to all meanings. This anxiety is aroused by the loss of a spiritual center, of an answer, however symbolic and indirect, to the question of the meaning of existence." [5] Because of the conditioning of his culture and the dereliction of those resources which witness against the denigration of selfhood, the search for selfhood, for responsible individuality, has, for many, become a crusade for atheistic individualism.

Underlying his struggle to find himself is the significant conviction of modern man that he must find himself in a world without God. This is the source of his deepest alienation. To be sure, he hides it from himself — obscures it with superficial activity and sentimental religion. But the image of himself reflected in his poetry, his plays, and his novels is one of terrible nakedness, and for the most part, one devoid of hope or grace. For him God is dead. He has cast his lot with the secular; his identity is tied to a this-world-only view of man.[6]

The Horatio Alger fable has become a part of the psychology of the twentieth century, but from the standpoint of status rather than the development of potentiality. Such a development is the logical consequence of the shallow concern of contemporary society for the individual and for the development of his potential for freedom and for service. Left thus alone, it is no wonder that modern man views himself as separated from both concern and community. He has no alternative, it would appear, but to regard himself as what Tillich and others have called him, "autonomous man — man alone." Although he can contend against many things, he cannot endure unrelieved loneliness. Because this is the specter that confronts him in modern technical civilization, "he seems willing in a Germany or a Russia or even in America, to sell his birthright of freedom for a porridge of hate, mistrust, and self-destruction." [7]

Perhaps the clearest voice that modern man seems to hear speaking directly to his situation and to him in particular is the political voice. It speaks with confidence, with concern and assurance, penetrating his loneliness and offering release from the prison of isolation. To the anxious and exhausted individual of the twentieth century, the sepulchral tones of Marx promise the end of the search, and the weak and weary soul is easy prey for the seduction. The power of the communist persuasion is a scientific power. It speaks to a scientific age of human dreams and community aspirations. It is both willing and able to use all the resources of its technology and psychology to seduce the individual and to persuade him, however falsely, of its willingness to assume his burden of care.

The rapid spread of communism may be attributed to many factors. Chief among these, however, we must count the desperate loneliness of isolated man in a world where the creations have outdistanced their creators and threaten mere human capacity for control. Automation has extended itself so far that at this writing there are in existence systems that enable one to dial for diagnosis and, even more frightening, that offer automated psychoanalysis! In the light of such developments and the prospect of more, it is not difficult to understand the surrender of an individual to a political philosophy of care, however false the claims of that philosophy may be. It is the logical result of the inability of the individual to find a sufficiently firm ground upon which to stand in any other system of thought. This system, however, like all systems that are based upon only an empirical and completely secular view of cosmic purpose and human potential, will, regardless of its claims, fail in its promise and ultimately know the consequences of its betrayal of the greater significance of responsible selfhood.

We ought not to underestimate the psychological effect of the statistical world picture; it displaces the individual in favor of anonymous units that pile up into mass formations. Science supplies us with, instead of the concrete individual, the names of organizations and, at the highest point, the abstract idea of the State as the principle of political reality. The moral responsibility of the individual is then inevitably replaced by the policy of the State (*raison d'état*). . . . The goal and meaning of individual life (which is the only *real* life) no longer lie in individual development but in the policy of the State, which is thrust upon the individual from outside and consists in the execution of an abstract idea which ultimately tends to attract all life to itself. The individual is increasingly deprived of the moral decision as to how he should live his own life, and instead is ruled, fed, clothed, and educated as a social unit, accommodated in the appropriate housing unit, and amused in accordance with the standards that give pleasure and satisfaction to the masses.[8]

The defection of many to communism within the present generation should not be counted so much a criticism of the individual as it should be counted a commentary upon the society from which the individual has "defected." The failure of the Christian church, for one, to recognize and redeem those weaknesses which are apparent in the secular culture is a mark of pastoral and educational reluctance and irrelevance. The nurturing responsibility and mission of the Christian community requires an awareness of not only the needs of the individual but of the dangers and temptations to which he or she is exposed. It demands, moreover, a willing courage to speak both in and to the cultural confusion.

The patterns described in the preceding pages are unquestionably patterns of frustration. Although they may appear as negative, they are positive insofar as they are signs that man cannot be content with what he makes of this world and this life. Man's continuing search, his seemingly blind movement from pillar to post, is actually a hopeful note in a world of compromise and surrender. It reveals a fundamental awareness on the part of the individual that there is more to life than what can be counted in terms of earthly possessions and community status. The basic fact that the individual knows he is as yet incomplete testifies to another dimension of the self yet to be discovered and appreciated.

What we have defined as confusion, Reinhold Niebuhr described as "mystery." He asserted that because "the self senses a mystery in itself and a mystery in the world beyond the flux of observable causes," it attempts to defeat what it senses as a threat "by finding that the one mystery, the ultimate or divine mystery, is a key to the understanding of the mystery of the self's transcendent freedom." [9]

Confronted by his existential frustration and failure and conscious of similar patterns among his contemporaries, the individual is virtually driven to the determination to discover and know himself. In this sense, he is the object of his own search for selfhood. He is, however, the one who does the seeking, and in that sense he is the subject of the search for selfhood. The ability of the individual to be both subject and object of the search for selfhood testifies to the capacity for self-transcendence. In the midst of futility at the existential level, this potential offers the key to the possibility of eventual recognition and resolution of the tension.

> That capacity of self-transcendence by which the self can become an object to itself is both the bearer of man's independence from the limits of nature and a reminder that one *becomes* human – he is not automatically endowed with humanity. Unlike the other animals, man does not become himself simply through biological maturation. The self is a development which emerges from the encounter between man the organism, man the ego, and man the member of society. It is a symbol of man's unique capacity to transcend the limited perspective of his own body.[10]

Man's search for himself is as dynamic as the self for which he searches. It flows from and develops in the life situations in which the individual is involved. If he is successful, therefore, the individual will find not so much a definition as he will a direction, an understanding, an integrating principle sufficiently broad and deep to encompass the various facets of his living and his hoping. It is a fallacy to presume that the essential integration of selfhood requires a completed view of life, a narrow and compact frame of reference. The truth of the matter is that "completed achievements leave us hollow and at loose ends. It is only the unfinished tasks that integrate and motivate." [11]

The emptiness experienced by modern man even after the most significant of secular accomplishments testifies to the shallowness and impermanence of temporal goals and ideals. Man's resultant discontent with and dissatisfaction over even an abundance of creature comforts bears out his need for a motivation from beyond this world yet relevant to it. The individual requires a sense of purpose that is of and true to himself, relevant to all the occasions of human life, yet not limited to them or bound by their control. The failure to recognize and accept this suprahuman dimension of personal need is the greatest weakness in any secular, political, or religious philosophy, regardless of its name or its claim. This is the greatest distinction between the needs of the individual and the false panacea offered by secular society in the form of the state. "Happiness and contentment, equability of soul and meaningfulness of life — these can be experienced only by the individual and not by a State, which, on the one hand, is nothing but a convention of independent individuals and, on the other, continually threatens to paralyze and suppress the individual." [12]

In the political realm, the pressure and concern of modern society are directed so strongly toward the national and international welfare that there is a tendency to neglect the permanent significance of the individual. The fact of the matter is that there can be no national or international solution to the problems of our day unless and until there is a personal resolution, for each human society is but a composite of the individuals who comprise it. The contemporary world scene reminds us that although history may enlarge the scope of the collective action that affects all individual destinies, it does not, according to Reinhold Niebuhr, " obviate any of the problems which the single self faces in its involvement in, and transcendence over, its collective destinies." [13]

Accustomed as we have become to talking in terms of the group or the mass, there is always the danger of forgetting or neglecting the individuality of those who constitute society. To the degree to which the individual is aware of himself and his significance, to that degree the group or groups of which he is a part will function properly and beneficially. To the degree to which the individual is submerged in or overcome by the mass, to that degree the group or organization will fail in both its immediate effectiveness and its long-range purpose. The complex structure of twentieth-century society must not be allowed to overshadow or override the concept of responsible selfhood as the root of all true community. If we expect society to behave in a mature and adult fashion, demonstrating the appropriate restraint and judgment, we must look for and develop such characteristics in the majority of its citizens. Stephen Neill asserts that despite his seeming unimportance, " by educating himself, the individual citizen is helping to determine the destinies of his nation and so of the world." [14]

The gnawing dissatisfaction of modern man with even the abundance of the goods, philosophies, and advantages of this world indicates the existence of a vacuum in his living. The anxiety that plagues the individual is a sign of his frustration and sense of incompleteness. In this sense, the " anxiety of meaninglessness " is positive, for it illustrates the fact that man has not yet completed his course, that he has not yet " arrived." It is this knowledge, albeit unwelcome and discomforting, that incites him to strive still further and to seek yet more demandingly for a deeper sense of personal significance than that offered by the secular society.

As man is able to recognize the source of his frustration, he is able to accept the possibility and, indeed, the necessity for self-transcendence. He begins to see that his successes or failures are not ultimately measured in terms of the things he has or has not gained, the worldly success he has or has not attained. Such failure as there may be in this world lies within himself, in his lack of a comprehensive and controlling purpose, of a relevant principle of integration. Such a purpose or principle will not only give meaning to his social relationships but will also provide an essential harmony for the conduct of the relationship he has with himself. It is, therefore, perhaps convenient to think of the individual "as a unified system with two sets of problems — one the problem of maintaining inner harmony within himself, and the other the problem of maintaining harmony with the environment, especially the social environment, in the midst of which he lives." [15]

The search for selfhood has three distinct and yet complementary aspects. The first of these is introspection. The individual seeks to discover the nature and significance of his selfhood through self-knowledge and self-evaluation. Out of this comes the concept of individuality, the realization that he differs from every other in peculiar strengths and weaknesses. The fullness of this knowledge defies definition because it is dynamic and not static, subject to change at every level and at every moment in response to the life situations in which it is developed. "The self is not its definition or description but rather the central being of the individual person. . . . Any verbal analysis tends to categorize or segment the self into communicable aspects or parts. The self can only be experienced." [16]

Any political, philosophical, or religious system, then, which fails to take into account the dynamic fullness of the self and attempts to affix a label on the basis of a moment or an incident in time or space must, of necessity, be inadequate and unsuitable. If the individual is constantly in the process of becoming, any definition of selfhood must be both broad and fluid enough to encompass not only the present reality but the future possibility.

The human self needs to be seen both for what it is at a given point in time, which is the existing self, and for what it may become in time, which is the potential self. Without the former we soon lapse into romantic, unrealistic pictures of secular or religious Utopias dwelt in by supermen and supersaints, such as were never seen and never will be. But without keeping in view what man may become we readily sink into cynicism or despair.[17]

The second aspect of the search for selfhood is man's need for relationship. " Selfhood is called into being through meeting and response. It will never be discovered as an isolated entity." [18] The individual requires someone to whom he can relate, with whom he can compare and contrast. The power of this need is reflected in modern society's concern for group activities and the emphasis on the part of the local churches on " group life " experiences. " The richness of human existence cannot be known in any individual, it can only be seen in the fullness of individualities. . . . Because men are unlike they need one another. Individuality is the natural presupposition of community; the natural fact that we need each other is, so to speak, the natural form of community." [19]

The weakness or failure of contemporary society in this area, indicated clearly in the main currents of modern literature and drama, is the tendency to receive the individual into relationship on a superficial level. There we find clearly demonstrated the incontrovertible fact that the mere presence of another is not sufficient. Crowded cities, the very citadels of alienation and loneliness regardless of the number of clubs and societies, testify mutely but strikingly to the fact that despite their best intentions, they are the servants of separation. What the individual seeks and needs is not " togetherness," but a deeper, more realistic and more elastic bond of mutual concern, interest, and acceptance. Thus the search for selfhood itself, if shared, becomes the means for meeting, for there is no concern more profound " than the desire to find oneself and to be a person in one's own right, regardless of age or status, regardless of poverty or wealth." [20]

Unless and until the fact of this deeper need is recognized and accepted, the individual will continue to be frustrated in his search for selfhood. Under superficial conditions, the height of his enthusiasm upon acceptance by a particular group is matched only by the depth of his disappointment and discouragement when the group is found to be insufficient and irrelevant. Such failure not only marks out the separation of the individual from his fellows (or furthers the already existing separation), but also indicates the separation he experiences within himself. In other words, the isolation forced upon the individual by a superficial concern for him alienates him not only from the group but from himself.[21]

The individual, then, who is the subject of the search for selfhood and the object of his own effort requires far more than the appearance of relationship and the semblance of community. He requires and deserves both the reality of a true community and the firm structure of relationships in which his particularity will be accepted and appreciated. Superficial community and the token of togetherness provides only milk when he requires strong meat. The community for which he seeks must be strong enough to receive and sustain his contribution and relevant enough to contribute its depth to his striving. It should be able to acknowledge and accept both his limitations and his potentialities, thus allowing for the full development of his selfhood. Such a community must have a dimension of depth as well as of breadth.

The relation of the individual to the community is a complex one which could be defined as consisting of vertical and horizontal dimensions. In the vertical dimension the individual is related to the community on two sharply contradictory forms. He looks up at the community as the fulfillment of his life and the sustainer of his existence. By its organization his physical and moral needs are met. . . . The individual looks down upon the community because he is, as it were, higher than it. It is bound to nature more inexorably than he. It knows nothing of a dimension of the eternal beyond its own existence. It therefore clings to its life desperately and may sacrifice every dignity to preserve its mere existence. The highest moral ideal to which it can aspire is a wise self-interest, which includes others in its ambition for security. Looking down at the community from his individual height the individual is embarrassed by the difference between the moral standards of the community and his own.[22]

Since the best of human communities falls short of achieving its potential and meeting and resolving the needs of its individual members, man must continue to seek for that which will give ultimate meaning to his selfhood. This is the third aspect of the search for selfhood and it may be defined as the need for an extramundane frame of reference. To withstand the pressures of the world and its society, such a perspective must have both its origin and its fulfillment *beyond* this world; yet to be relevant to man and his striving and seeking, it must be immediately involved and effective *in* this world. Man's capacity for self-transcendence implies the existence of such a context, and the possibility of its availability for his participation therein.

One of the fundamental truths of selfhood is that the individual self is both great and small, and the former aspect cannot be contained or fully expressed in the latter. " It can only realize itself by endlessly being drawn out of itself into larger ends. The community may provisionally be that end. But it cannot be so ultimately. For the community is, though broader than the individual, also much closer to the necessities of nature than it. The individual must have a higher end than the community." [23]

Self-transcendence means that the human creature, who is in nature and subject to nature, is able also at the same time to transcend nature. He dwells in the finite world of nature which cradles him. And yet he dwells also in a realm of spirit.

The realm of spirit is itself a realm which transcends physical nature in the sense that it is made up of intangibles. For while we live rooted in physical nature and dependent upon it, we are equally and perhaps even more dependent upon intangibles which, as far as can be discerned, have no physical existence. But for a given self these intangibles *do* exist. They can come and go, shrink or grow in importance, be found and be lost. The self may pine for the want of them, or suffer when he faces them, or exult when he possesses them or when they lay hold on him.[24]

That which the individual senses but cannot prove, that which he experiences but cannot define, testifies to the reality of this third dimension which is *for* but not *of* this world. It bespeaks a concept of and purpose for the self greater than that of any secular community. It is, however, relevant to and meaningful for every community. It is the truth of God for human life, made known in Jesus Christ and communicated through his body, the church.

## *Chapter Three*

# THE RESPONSE OF CHRISTIAN EDUCATION

When the individual realizes both the need for and the nature of his three-dimensional search for selfhood, he begins to seek for a community in which this totality is acknowledged and in which there is the promise of its nurture. Understanding that " it is possible to have an attitude to the external conditions of life only when there is a point of reference outside them," [1] the individual may come, in the course of his seeking, to the threshold of the Christian community. The apparent frustration of modern man and the persistence of his continuing search is a clear call to Christian education to speak to the situation out of the fullness of the revelation of God's care and concern most clearly made known in Jesus Christ.

Modern man recognizes with his inner sight the inadequacy of his own temporal and short-term solutions to the problem he faces — to the problem he is. As has been pointed out earlier, he is alert and responsive to any voice that will speak in and to his situation of a power and a purpose that is relevant to his need. Such a full perspective as man needs to make sense of his living and his striving can be derived only from his participation in and relationship to the divine, the eternal Lord of all life. The communication of this in the light of and with reference to the existential situation is the nurturing responsibility of Christian education, and man's ultimate hope of resolving his frustration and anxiety.

The simple, terrible truth of secular humanism is that man cannot affirm his own humanity. His anxiety is such that he is unable to distinguish between his own self-affirmation and his manipulation or abuse of other persons. The testimony of a shaking, quaking agnostic secularism is that " man cannot be *for* himself except in commitment to a community of faith in which both the immediacies of his becomings and the ultimate truth of his being are held in creative tension. Man affirms himself within the affirming love of God." [2]

The assurance for which man seeks and which he so desperately needs is the substance of God's historical self-revelation. This eternal truth, empirically verified in the historical action recited in the Biblical drama complements and completes earthly relationships and illuminates the dark corners of self-evaluation. The communication of this truth-in-revelation, the presentation of its relevance to the existential situation, is the vital core of the Christian community's educational activity. The importance of this aspect of nurturing responsibility was emphasized by Lewis Sherrill when he defined it as the " crucial element in the life of the Christian community and in the philosophy of Christian education. Indeed, it could be maintained that it is the determinative element in both." [3]

This third dimension truly expands the boundaries of human perspective. It illuminates and provides the comprehensive frame of reference for the enterprise of individuality, the full exercise of selfhood. It reveals not only the purpose of living, but illuminates the pathway to eventual achievement. The Christian revelation is intensely personal in both approach and purpose. It is relevantly individualistic. " The essence of revelation as God's self-disclosure is the movement of the divine Self toward the human self, and the essence of the movement of the divine Self is its redemptive purpose." [4]

As will be surveyed in Part II, from the second to the twentieth centuries developments within Christian education would appear to have replaced the element of personal concern demonstrated *by* Jesus with a concern for the communication or transmission of information *about* him. Viewed pastorally, this has resulted in a tendency to minimize the possibility of personal encounter while developing an interest in and a technique of communicating past history. Transmission of content is certainly of importance, but the primary concern of Christian education must be in the area of preparation for the culminating event, the personal encounter between man and God. " Christian education must be personal; it must take place in a personal encounter *and, only secondarily, is it transmissive.*" [5]

The " liberal theology " of the late nineteenth and early twentieth centuries signified an awareness on the part of the leaders of the movement for a revitalization of relevant human concern in the work of Christian education. Caught up by the movement later known as the " social gospel," they sought to implement their researches through the medium of the class or the group rather than the specific individual. Thus although the concern of the church has been more *humanly* centered during the past half century, it has still fallen short of the mark of *individual* concern established by the teaching ministry of Jesus.

A significant truth that needs to be returned to the forefront of the thinking of Christian education is that only to the degree to which the individual is aware of the possibility of an encounter with the living God can there be the possibility of a conversion that will affect the totality of his being. It is for such a personal confrontation that Christian education must prepare the individual. It must as well prepare the community of the faithful to receive and nurture this individual after the encounter has taken place. The full realization of not only the possibility but the depth of such an encounter is essential if Christian education is to perform relevantly its nurturing responsibility. For too long " conversion has taken place at the level of the current conscience of the community and has changed individuals so that they lived up to the highest current standards more completely. It has usually not included or involved any fundamental reconstruction of life in opposition to and beyond the best of the current ideology." [6]

The nature and type of confrontation and conversion that is a vital and proper part of the Christian tradition is not a matter of convenience or status. It is, in fact and experience, a matter of " psyche-shaking " reality and power.

When a man encounters the Self-revealing God he is confronted, not by a release of fresh divine information to be digested, not by some new and infallible dogma about God, not by a list of new rules to be observed or old ones to be furbished up again; he is confronted by none of these trappings of religion and church-craft, but by a Person who offers himself to us in love and judgment, and calls upon us to give ourselves a living sacrifice in response. It is a matter of personal communion. If this is the core of revelation, so must it be the core of Christian education.[7]

Thus the nurturing activity of Christian education, when it is true to the example and commission of its Lord, and constantly sensitive to his presence, is both aware of and alert to the individual and his needs. As the confrontation with God is personal, so must be the nature and quality of the educational activity of the Christian community both before and after the event. The self furthers and is furthered by the community of which it is a responsible and expressive part. The revelation of God's eternal and particular love for each child illuminates and inspires both selfhood and relationship. The end result is the Christian community in which the three aspects of selfhood are valued and fostered. This is the type of community referred to in the New Testament as koinonia.

" *Koinonia* is a kind of community which transcends ordinary human community in that God is present and participant in the community. . . . Thus it signifies that every relationship in the Christian community participates in God and God in it, whether it be the relationship of person to person, or of each to all, or all to each." [8] It is a community of the Spirit, and only such a community as this is sufficiently broad and strong to meet the needs of individuals in a world at war between the powers of light and the powers of darkness. The significant weakness in the formal movement known as Christian education has been its apparent inability to see the forest for the trees. It has allowed itself to become specialized in the poorest — the limited — sense of the term. In the mind and experience of man, " Christian education " is a mysterious something of no particularly vital significance directed by elderly ladies and gentlemen for the very young and naïve, and usually takes place in makeshift rooms and dusty basements of church buildings. It is defined and evaluated in terms of where and when it meets, and represents, for many, a Sunday morning sitter service. The truth of the matter is that " there is no experience which does not have an influence on what people become. And if religion is concerned with all phases of life, then most of life's experiences may be thought of as the religious curriculum." [9]

The significance of the type of community which is of the essence of the Christian tradition and the Christian promise for an age in which conformity is too easily mistaken and too quickly adopted as an acceptable substitute has been enunciated by Martin Marty:

> In the Christian witness the picture of man in community is brought further into focus under a new covenant — the " man in Christ " sharing the common life in the Body of Christ. Ecclesiology and anthropology have been fused in the study of the New Testament description of the *koinonia,* the shared life. Here the horizontal relations of man to men are characterized by participation in the divine life which is a gift from Christ (a vertical relationship). Here there grows a partnership of loving service and unity which draws its strength from the remembrance of Jesus Christ and the contemporaneity of his gifts.[10]

This is no " group " action, save in its most occasional and most sophisticated moments. It is fundamentally individualistic. The community as it is created and as it creates is based on " two poles or foci; namely, man and God. The two encounter each other and interact with each other so that they are drawn together or draw further apart according to the nature of the relationship set up between them during the encounter." [11] The community as it results and responds is but the sum total of the particular God-to-man and man-to-God relationships contained therein.

In no sense, then, can the Christian community be considered as a refuge or a retreat from the pressures and demands of human life. It is not an isolated society removed from or free of the tensions and temptations of the existential society in which it lives and in which it exerts its leavening influence. To the contrary, unless and until that community is, through both its particular individualities and its combined relationships, thoroughly involved in the world it cannot be true to its commission or faithful over its stewardship. This is a vital principle which must be placed in the highest priority of the Christian educative endeavor. There must be on the part of the individual and the group both the willingness and the courage to go into the world bearing the "good news," the charity and compassion to receive the world, and the perspective to interpret the world to itself.

The dual awareness of world and witness must be a conscious part of every effort in the educational and pastoral mission. As the world must be brought into the curriculum and the concern, so must the gospel be brought into the world in order that the Christian community may speak with both clarity and compassion to all men in all situations out of cultural awareness and Christian responsibility. Where the church is effective in its mission and true to its mandate, it does to some degree take "on the character of its day . . . , and its theology tends to speak the language of the day. At the same time, the church is concerned with the culture in a creative way. It has a mission to the culture of the day that is critical, constructive, and reconstructive. The church always reflects and remakes the culture in which it lives." [12]

The church is able to do this with effectiveness only by virtue of the guiding presence of its Lord and its conscious devotion to his will and service. By its prayers, by its "Practice of the Presence of God," the Christian community aligns itself, as it were, with the plumb line of eternal significance which alone provides the measure for the proper perspective on the cultural situation. What God wills as well as what God is, is an essential element in the revelatory action in and upon the church. Thus the church in every age sees what it is and what it is called to be. "*The Christian community by virtue of its own nature is in the unique position of being a true community of living persons, but of being able also at the same time to stand above itself and view itself under the light of revelation and eternity.*" [13]

Out of this context the Christian community is able to minister directly to the individual with particular concern for the full acceptance and development of his selfhood. It can, as well, speak convincingly to the secular community of which the individual is a part, revealing something of the full depth and purpose of the Christian community as a society of free persons, characterized by a horizontal concern for mutual benefit and a vertical directive and incentive. By its responsible ability to be true to the self-revelation of God and to communicate to man his particular opportunity for participation in that revelatory benefit and action, Christian education nurtures and prepares the individual for not only effective living in this world, but significant living in the light of an eternal purpose. No other community can minister so significantly, for no other community is so informed and inspired by the threefold revelation of the creating, redeeming, sanctifying God who meets and succors the individual in his search for selfhood.

Christianity sees a more ultimate root of human community than secularism can offer. It believes with secularism that there are important bonds of community in the social nature of persons. Within the empirical context of human existence there are vital resources for the achievement of a large degree of fellowship. Nevertheless, the Christian frame of man provides a more ultimate ground of interdependence. Christian faith claims that all persons are children of one family in God. The ultimate bond of Christian community is therefore supra-social.[14]

The importance of this central fact cannot be overlooked in any relevant and/or redemptive program of Christian education and pastoral care. An appreciation of it, however, in both its fullness and its strength, is possible only out of an awareness of its historical development. Therefore, it is necessary to turn to a recapitulation of Christian education and its development from the personal, pastoral ministry of Jesus to the present pattern.

# II

# CHRISTIAN EDUCATION IN HISTORY AND PRACTICE

*O Jerusalem, Jerusalem, which killest the prophets, and stonest them that are sent unto thee; how often would I have gathered thy children together, as a hen doth gather her brood under her wings, and ye would not!*

— Luke 13:34.

## *Chapter Four*

# THE PATTERN OF TEACHING

The role of the Christian church in nurture and in education as in all other areas of its concern is based upon the existential experience of its Lord and Master, Jesus Christ, in relation to those with whom he walked and talked. The encounter between the Jesus of history and those who personally confronted him established not a methodology but a reality of pattern and purpose out of which came a sense of the mark toward which all those who took his cross must strive. By word, by deed, through " conversation by gesture " he communicated to men, women, and children the full implication of their separated plight and the genuine assurance of God's love and concern for them as individuals. The response he met was engendered by his recognition of reality. His redemptive actions were relevant to the basic realities of human life. His most penetrating regard was for the individual who sincerely sought release from all the captivity that made of him less than he was created to be.

It is to this ministry, in the richness of both its motive and its efficacy, that Christian education must look as it seeks to determine the proper and enduring foundation for its nurturing activity. As Jesus in his ministry went beyond and below the level of physical impairment to the vital depth of disease, even so must the church that bears his sign go beyond and below " approaches," " techniques," and " laboratories " if it, in its turn, is to be relevant and redemptive. The personalness and sense of immediacy demonstrated in the ministry of Jesus bespeak his relationship with the Father, the touchstone of his nurturing activity. "Jesus said to them, 'Truly, truly, I say to you, the Son can do nothing of his own accord, but only what he sees the Father doing; for whatever he does, that the Son does likewise.'" (John 5:19.) The earliest Gospels emphasize the immediate and personal relationship between Jesus and God the Father and lead us to believe without question that this was also true of the relationships Jesus enjoyed with the early Christians.[1]

It is true that in the present day even the designation, "Jesus of history," is questioned because of its adoption by a particular school of thought. The course of history indicates that all too often Jesus has been identified with mortal schools of thought rather than vice versa. The historical Jesus was such that both the Gnostics and the Pelagians laid claim to his succession. He has been so "liberalized" that he is, in some circles, no more awe-inspiring than the playmates of one's young child! He has, on the other hand, been so "eschatologized" that the prospect of confrontation implies no compassion and incites only terror.

Somewhere between these poles lies the truth, and such a glimmer of it as we are permitted so long after the fact is due in no small measure to the researches of archaeologists, cultural anthropologists, and form critics. Both oral and written traditions coalesce at a point movingly described by Stephen Neill:

> The Jesus who strides through the Gospels is a man of immense and terrifying power. He is the master of every situation. He speaks with authority and not as the scribes. He is never at a loss for an answer. His glance can quell and put to flight the crowds of buyers and sellers in the Temple. He knows how to draw men and women to himself in a devotion which will prove stronger than persecution and death.[2]

We have, then, the picture of One who came not to deny or destroy either the Law or the Prophets but to fulfill their work and their effort. He is the One who brings to historical reality the promise made to Abraham and his seed forever. He is One whose teaching goes beyond that of patriarch, judge, king, or prophet. He exceeds the scribes in both wisdom and authority because he is dedicated, not to a function in the narrow sense of the term, but to an action rooted in grace and nourished in the infinite wisdom of the Father's everlasting intention. The " teaching " of Jesus was not a matter of pericope or parable. These were methods, it is true, but so was the team of four who bore the paralytic, the funeral cortege in the city of Nain, and a herd of swine, to mention but a few. There was no " proper " time or place in the ministry of Jesus, for all times and places were sanctified to the end for which he came. Thus his teaching was a vital component of and derivative of his seeing, his hearing, *his total participation in the total experience of those for whom he became flesh and among whom he dwelt.*

Sensitive as he was to the questing doubt of first-century Jewry, alert as he was to the genuine desire not so much for wealth, for power, and for riches on the part of his historical contemporaries as for the substantiating truth of a suspected dignity of self, he went among them as one who serves, distinguishing between the shallow and the sacred, the hollow and the holy, concerned for the cure, not merely of bodies, but of souls. Thus the context of his teaching was the complex of human life, its heights and its depths, its triumphs and its trivialities. He delays a party to care for a stomachache, he arbitrates a dispute between sisters, he pauses a march to death to minister to a blind beggar, and he ceases his own dying to assure a habitual criminal of entry into paradise.

In the historical record, Jesus is to be seen continually meeting people in the midst of their various occupations and secular pursuits. There, on their ground, he reveals the concern of God for their difficulties, their frustrations, and their failures. He speaks to farmers in terms of farms and crops, to women in terms of women's work, and to clergy in terms of the Law and the Prophets. The specific situation in which he found himself was recognized and accepted for what it was, addressed and ministered to in terms of what it could be in the light of the redemptive love of God. This was a ministry to need. It was pastoral teaching on the ground of realism, of existential concern. This was no ministry guided by what would be deemed acceptable by acceptable people. The guidelines of this ministry were those of love and conviction, not likableness and convenience. Although it is dangerous to generalize, in the clinical sense there is much truth in the following description of his word and work:

> The whole message of Jesus was addressed to the alienated, excommunicated, and disassociated conditions within the commonwealth of the spiritual community. He felt keenly the wideness of the fixed gulf between the outcasts and those whose legalistic safety measures had excommunicated them. He affirmed the power of his love to establish community with them again, without at the same time excusing them from the fixed fact of their sinfulness. He manifested that perfect love which would cast out their fear of punishment whereby law would be overcome by grace.[3]

This Jesus, then, in history opens to man the possibility of restoration to the relationship with God for which he was created and the relationship with man which is incumbent upon the child of God. Through both his personality and his personal involvement in the affairs of men this Jesus clarifies the distinction between good and evil, offers to each individual the privilege of choice, and culminates his ministry with the witness that good is not overcome of evil. There is in this ministry an evident awareness of both God's will and man's way. " He is, for us, not only the revelation of the nature of God but also the revelation of the nature of man." [4]

The involvement of Jesus of Nazareth in the lives and circumstances of his time witnesses to the highly individualized concern of God for each of his children *in particular.* No person is too ill with an illness of either the body or the spirit for his healing touch. No person is too exalted and none too humble (cf. the rich young man who " went away sorrowful," and the publican who " beat his breast ") for his relevant proclamation of the will of God concerning that individual. The sensitivity of the historical Jesus to the needs of individuals, his communication in unmistakable terms of the concern of God for the satisfaction of needs both seen and unseen, bear out the concern for self-development as a cardinal aim of the educational, the nurturing, endeavor. In his work and witness, Jesus combines a realization of the existential situation with a revelation of the nature and purpose of God to the benefit of the particular individual to whom he is ministering at the given moment. The implications of this activity reach far beyond the limits of his physical touch or the sound of his voice. The realm of his activity is not merely the present; it is past and future as well, for in himself he reveals both God and man.

As the personal revelation of God, Jesus can only be known, with full certainty, because He unveils not only God's true Being, but also the reality and truth of human existence. Knowledge of Christ is at the same time self-knowledge. Jesus not only reveals what God is, and what He wills, but He reveals at the same time that we are sinners, that we are opposed to our origin and our divinely created nature. In His Person Jesus reveals true God and true Man; and since He reveals true Man He unveils the falsity of our actual state, our existence-in-untruth, our sinful condition. Jesus reveals true human existence as existence in the love of God.[5]

This, then, is the pattern, for the individual-centered ministry of Jesus served to provide the context in which the community of the children of God could develop and function. The privileges and responsibilities of membership in this family are made plain by the constant refrain, " Go, and do thou likewise." The injunction to share and extend the gift received, the relationship experienced, the acceptance acknowledged, was a not-always-tacit implication in the nurturing activity of Jesus. " The love which is revealed in Christ is a love which seeks the fulfillment of all things in such a relationship to one another that what flows from the life of each enriches the life of all, and each participant in the whole life finds his own good realized through the giving of self to the life of the whole." [6]

The beginning, however, is with the realization of both the nature and the responsibilities of selfhood. This is demonstrated most clearly in the relationship between Jesus and each of his disciples. Acknowledging and accepting the limitations of their respective understandings, he nonetheless was sensitive and sympathetic to their sincere desire to respond, and to each was given the appropriate counsel. The rebuke of Simon Peter at Caesarea Philippi was a rebuke of love, not of dismissal. The subsequent denials and desertion of the same Peter, the youthful egocentric questioning of James and John, the seemingly desperate honesty of the doubting Thomas — all these are recognized as part of the searching activity, as adolescent gropings for spiritual maturity, the temporary and transient evidences of as yet imperfect comprehension. The ministry to these, the education of these, is in the context of mortal limitation, yet with the power and the promise of a transformation finally realized by those who watched and waited at Pentecost.

The confusion and concern that occupied the disciples following the events at the palace, on Golgotha, and in the tomb of Joseph of Arimathea is evident not so much by what is recorded in the three accounts as by what is not recorded. The indecision of the group, their individual and corporate sense of inadequacy, is quite apparent in the absence of any account of significant activity. Despite the conversion, the conversation, and the companionship each of them had enjoyed with Jesus, his departure from this world left them apparently leaderless. What God in Christ had done for them, he had done for them on a personal, a highly individualistic, basis. They shared in common only a similarity of encounter with a particular Person. They were as spokes in the wheel, each contributing to the strength of the whole, but uncertain as to what held them together. Not one of them presumed to take the place of Jesus, although it would appear that they looked at first to Peter as the oldest and closest to Jesus for directions and instructions. Mindful of his betrayal, however, and unsure in his own mind and faith, Peter was most reluctant to assume this responsibility.

But suddenly — just as suddenly as the " wind " that filled the place where they all were on that day gathered — they knew what had to be done and who was to do it. The promised outpouring of the Holy Spirit enabled them to comprehend the nature of the ministry that had been passed into their hands, the work of interpretation that was from thenceforth their several and combined vocations. They were not leaderless, for God had raised Jesus up and of that they were all witnesses. Therefore what they had seen and shared was now to be told, now to be practiced, now to be proclaimed, for that truth was their testimony and the communication of it their solemn task.

Thus it was that following the strange events in the upper room, a change came over the Christian community as it began to be known and make its influence felt. Where Jesus had healed the sick in both body and soul, the disciples began to concentrate on what the modern age might call " preventive spiritual medicine." Following him and his practice they remained disciples. Yet now they were as well apostles, ones who were sent bearing a message. The transformation from disciples to apostles, the difference in function, is the key to understanding the first significant development in Christian education and pastoral care after the historical ministry of Jesus. What these men had seen and shared, what they had personally experienced and encountered, they now told abroad. Previously, men, women, and children had sought out Jesus, primarily for healing. After Pentecost the apostles sought out men, women, and children to tell them what God had done in Christ. Although many to whom they spoke had seen and known Jesus, the emphasis now changed from confrontation to communication. Along with the work of proclamation and as a natural consequence of it there developed a specific concern for teaching, for instruction, for the spelling out of the historical events with particular reference to the individual. Highly influenced by an apocalyptic sense, the apostles soon developed a basic pattern and content of instruction. Gradually there evolved certain general statements and guidelines of conduct concerning the expected deportment and regulation of the lives that accepted the historical action of Jesus as revelatory truth for their adoption and emulation.[7]

To understand better the nature of the apostolic function, it can be viewed from the perspective of its component parts: the proclamation of the " good news," the core of the gospel, the *kērygma,* that " God was in Christ reconciling the world to himself," and the *didachē,* the teaching of the implications of that action in the lives of men. In one sense, the relationship between these two parts is syllogistic. The *kērygma* initiates and informs the *didachē*. It results in what T. O. Wedel has called " the ethic of therefore." Because God was in Christ, and because this was perceived by men, therefore . . . We see this most clearly defined and presented in its most sophisticated form in the Pauline letters. It marks the beginning of the Christian educational tradition in its formal aspect, and " it both formed and was formed by the earliest Christian groups in Jerusalem and in the Greco-Roman world of the first century." [8]

One prime characteristic of the ministry of Jesus was his concern for the individual. The relevance of his teaching to particular situations was unmistakable. His preaching was done, as was his healing, in the context of immediacy. The apostles attempted to follow suit in their presentation of that life and its meaning for those lives which had seen or heard of it. Any real development of selfhood must, in the final analysis, take place in a one-to-one relationship, and the effort of the apostles was to bring men and women to the point of understanding from which they could establish — or reestablish — such a relationship with the Father through the work of the Son by the assurance of the Holy Spirit. Thus the *personal* aspect of the nurturing, the educational task, remained in the forefront of the apostolic effort, even though groups began to replace individuals as the focus of instruction. The shift from individual confrontation to group communication was necessitated in part by the zeal of the apostles to bring to as many as possible the " good news " of what God had done in Christ. It was occasioned also by the desire on the part of individuals to hear firsthand about the Jesus of history who made the lame walk, the blind see, and contended with the scribes and Pharisees. At the same time, the political and ecclesiastical suspicion of the new heresy caused the Christians to meet together in cells or groups to reaffirm their allegiance in concert and to deepen in companionship their conviction and their commitment. At the heart of the movement, however, remained the concern for the individual, and on the part of the individual was the increasing awareness that he was the distinct subject of God's never-failing love and care.

Thus the concern for individuality, for self-realization, for self-development, to which the *kērygma* testified, was implemented and informed by the *didachē,* wherein the implications of selfhood were presented in the light of contemporary issues and responsibilities. The work and witness of Jesus was thereby extended and amplified during the apostolic period, for the efforts of the apostles in their preaching and teaching activities were directed to the same end as those of Jesus in his ministry: " that persons might be drawn into the kingdom of God; that they might attain to increasing self-understanding and self-knowledge and an increasing realization of their own potentialities; and that they might sustain the relationships and responsibilities of life as children of God." [9]

## *Chapter Five*

# EXPANSION AND SOLIDIFICATION

The new heresy (as it was known by its opponents), or the new religion (as it was professed by its followers), called Christianity spread rapidly across the country of its birth and the world of its time. Although the mighty acts of the carpenter's son of Nazareth soon passed into the historical lore, the significant and continuing actions of his followers did not, but provided new evidence of a strange power and purpose at work in the world of men. Empowered by the Spirit of God and reassured by the testimony of an empty tomb that they counted a victory, the apostles and an increasing number of converts exercised a ministry that was both faithful and far-reaching. Within a few years after the mysterious and dramatic events centered in Jerusalem, there were cells, underground communities of Christians, in almost every major city of the Near East. Pressured and persecuted in a variety of ways, the reaction and resistance of these Christians to the civil and religious power of the world, to the temptations of body and spirit, provoked reluctant admiration and strong antagonism among their contemporaries. As individuals and as a group, they appeared to have a strength of mysterious origin, certainly from beyond this world, one that enabled them not only to confront and withstand temporal power and accepted religious custom but to convert such effort and witness to a more humble and lasting concern.

Underlying this work and this witness was, of course, the

conviction that God had spoken to them as individuals and had called each of them into a new relationship with him, a relationship of such lasting love and power that not even the fear of imprisonment, torture, and death could destroy their devotion and its manifestation, their discipleship. In its early stages Christianity continued to draw heavily from Judaism for its converts, perhaps because it represented a completion of their preparation and anticipation. In some instances, the communication of the love of God for the individual, made known through the Person of Jesus the Christ, provided a welcome release from the bonds of a legalistic and somewhat impersonally centered religion of custom and code. In other instances, the freedom implied in the " good news " sparked a " revolt against the confining influences of the ark which was claimed to be the only true dwelling place of the shining presence of God." [1]

This recognition of distinction in the sight of God, of particularity in his love, drew men and women to the apostles and to the arenas to learn and bear witness to the sincerity of their search and the gratitude for what God had done for them in Christ. In both cases, however, the response was free and willingly given, despite the expense of the consequences. The apostolic proclamation, the *kērygma,* was directed to all men, yet it was presented relevantly to each man in the light and context of his particular situation and experience. The preaching of the early Christians was not so much interpretive or catechetical as it was factual. The individual could sense and see in such a recital the measure of his or her own blindness, the consequence of an acknowledged hardness of heart, and the opportunity for cleansing and restoration offered through recognition and repentance. With such a foundation it is easy to understand why the *didachē,* the teaching concerning implication and implementation, should also focus on a strongly personal emphasis. It evolved out of a context of " I " rather than " they," and centered on self-integrity and personal responsibility rather than on group image and corporate concern. In his encounter with the proclamation and his exposure to the teaching, the individual recognized himself as singled out, particularized, distinguished either positively or negatively — and sometimes both — for perhaps the first time in his existence. By virtue of the relevance to him and his situation of the early preaching and teaching, by virtue of the realism and the release offered in the "good news," the individual responded in sincere gratitude and personal commitment to that which acknowledged him and assured the significance of his selfhood. The importance of the twin factors of relevance and realism cannot be overemphasized, particularly in the historical context.

Christianity satisfied both the religious and philosophic instincts of the time. It offered a cultus in which the individual found his own personal needs and the desire for brotherhood in worship satisfied. This cultus shared with others the merit of giving the realization of the means of salvation; it was superior in that the Savior was not merely a figure of unique attraction, but also a recent historical figure invested with deity — not a mythological personage encumbered with legends which to many thinking men were positively offensive and to others were at least in need of defense; it was superior in that the salvation involved was a salvation from forces of moral evil, and in that the cultus itself was simple and free from primitive ritual survivals in need of allegorical explanations.[2]

Throughout this period of definition and expansion, there remained at the center of the Christian witness to the world the high doctrine of the individual personality, the self. The followers of Jesus maintained his practice and sought to duplicate his pastoral concern and personal involvement in nurture. Within the Christian groups as they were formed there developed a new kind of community, one in which the individual was not absorbed or overcome, but in which he or she was encouraged to maintain the gift of individuality and to give it expression. Indeed, the individual was stimulated to nurture the seed of this gift for the benefit of others, for the dual benefit of the self and the society of which it was a part. These Christian cells were characterized by the fact that they were " a society of persons, infinitely worthful, freed and equal before God, and subject to God's will as revealed through Christ and through the Spirit." [3]

The relevant and realistic communication of the privileges and responsibilities of individuality drew men and women out of their weak and subjugated religious and political conformity into the grateful acceptance and bold assumption of full selfhood under God. The message of the apostles was a personal message, directed to specific cultural, political, social, economic, and religious practices as they influenced the lives of persons. The promise of the apostles was of a new *quality* of life that would transform and transcend whatever the *quantity* of that life had been. The personal acceptance of the truth of God in Christ, as it was proclaimed by the apostles through the power of the Holy Spirit, resulted in an awareness of the significance of individuality and the nature of the community in which that individuality could be received and upheld to the strengthening of the whole and the nurture of its component parts. Without this personal acceptance of Jesus the Christ and the resultant personal loyalty in the form of discipleship, there could be neither entrance into nor participation in the Christian community, but the results far outweighed the sacrifice. " This meant a new life in the Christian group, in which each person felt himself to hold a trust for all his fellow members. It was a bond stronger than the natural ties of family, culture, race, tribe, or nation." [4]

In such a society, however, where the individual was accepted and acknowledged in the fullness of both background and potential, it soon became necessary to define in relevant and consistent terms the anticipated conduct of subsequent life in this world. This was, it is true, the responsibility of the individual in the light of his or her acceptance into the community, but the community had, in turn, to clarify and enunciate certain standards of conduct and concern. The teaching that then began to develop was based firmly on the realization of the nature of selfhood and the concern for the good use of man's birthright as revealed by Jesus the Christ. The sense of personal relationship to God and individual responsibility to one's neighbor — Christian, Jew, or pagan — was the continuing dynamic of the group in which this individuality became community. It manifested itself in contrast to the secular community by an "outreaching" rather than an "indrawing" emphasis, and this implementation of the dynamic, what we now call evangelistic activity, soon developed into one of the prime concerns on the part of both the Christian community as a whole and its individual members. Thus throughout this period there was a gradual development of both consciousness and concern, of acknowledgment and activity, that came out of practical experience and personal devotion. The Christian ethic as it came to be known "developed within living communities of men, women, and children, essentially such as any of us knows today. The love for which it called, and the illustrative virtues of self-control and all the rest, were directed toward persons just as easy and just as difficult to be neighbors with, as any of us." [5]

With the expansion of Christianity, however, and its eager reception and adoption by increasing numbers of people, the opportunity for individual instruction and supervision by one of the Twelve became less and less possible. In the interest of both unity of effort and faithfulness of response, the several Christian communities had to work out definitions and boundaries by means of which to describe and define themselves and their purpose in the light of both Christian and cultural patterns of thought and activity. A natural result of the process of definition is limitation and restriction, and the Christian communities were not immune to this danger. The sequence is clear: out of encounter comes evangelism, which not only involves but results in education that culminates in establishment.

The center of this educational mission of the early church was the personal relationship between God and the individual, informed now not only by those who had encountered

Jesus in the flesh but by those who had encountered him in the Spirit. Certain convictions were held in concert, and from these there grew a distinguishable pattern of behavior and concern that defined as its foundation a particular concept of man's relationship to his Father and his brethren. The general acceptance and experience of this norm soon resulted in its adoption as an expected culmination and consequence. From this point, it was but a short step to the development of a custom and a code that became the substitute for personal confrontation and commitment as the qualification for membership in the Christian fellowship. Commitment in the personal sense thus began to be replaced by custom, code, and conformity in the intellectual sense.

One of the earliest teaching devices and one that perhaps speeded this change from personal commitment to intellectual conformity, was the epistle. From the leaders of the church at Jerusalem and from some of the more pastorally minded of the apostles in the field, letters were sent, from time to time, to specific places in answer to specific questions about the relationship between Christianity and the culture. The concern of the writers was to impart the basic denominator of the Christian faith in the light of cultural backgrounds and customs. The letters were so effective, however, that they were exchanged and shared, and thereby contributed to a unanimity that may have been helpful at the time but that was also dangerously close to the brink of conformity.

The involvement of individual Christians and the local communities of Christians in the affairs of the secular society from which they had been called and to which they believed themselves sent did pose certain difficulties. To what extent was the Christian group to become involved, and what form should its involvement take? There was no pattern to which either the individual or the group could refer. Each situation was new, something of a crisis; it called for prayerful consideration of the needs of men in the light of the purpose of God. By such recognition and by such wrestling the church grew — but not without pain. There were occasions of disparity and disagreement, notable among which was the conflict between Paul and the leaders of the church at Jerusalem. In the final analysis, however, and viewed from the larger perspective of subsequent history, we can see that this was good for the church and contributed to its strength. The lack of a pattern, the absence of a well-charted course, permitted the exercise of individuality and self-responsibility that fostered both relevance and immediacy of concern. It demonstrated on the social level the comprehensive particularity of the Father's concern and love for his children. Out of such personal confidence, then, but certainly not without trepidation, individuals — singly and together — responded in faithful action. Thus what had seemed to be the problem was recognized as potential and what had been defined as indecision was accepted as inspiration.

The Kingdom of God by its nature required a society where its ethic should be lived, and that society is the church; but just as the ethic is not delivered with legalistic precision, so also the church as the society where the ethic is to govern men is not delivered by Jesus in finished form. It would have been as alien to him to do the one as to do the other. And by the same token it is of the nature of His Spirit to guide the development of both the Church and the ethic, the one as truly as the other; for both the church and the ethic are meant to be embodiments of his Spirit. They are the society and the Law, respectively, of those who are sons of God through faith in Jesus Christ. The church itself is the Christian social order, or shall we say, it becomes that in proportion as the ethic of the Kingdom of God is lived in the church.[6]

All this serves to point up the educational challenge confronting the early church: to maintain the concept of individuality while proclaiming the common ground for community regardless of religious background or culture. The acceptance of the reconciling activity of God is, however, immediately followed by the question as to what is then expected, desired by God of those who have made this act of faith. Thus the formal function and responsibility of teaching early became essential to the maintenance and extension of the religion. From the beginning, teaching was a necessary complement to the evangelistic activity of the apostles. The combination was essential because "for the Jews, the Hebrew Scriptures required re-interpretation. Where men were less acquainted with the Hebrew faith, there was need of a more elementary instruction." [7]

The readiness and appreciation for this type of religious education is apparent in the rapid and enthusiastic reception it received. The spread of the Christian gospel and the rapidity of its adoption by individuals is significant testimony not only to its truth but to the needs of man, for whom it was given. The religiopolitical climate was indeed favorable to its individual reception, and the desire for social reform was strong. "Christianity came on the crest of a wave; it was able to use and direct existing tendencies. If it seemed unoriginal in ethics, still it was able to give a new motive for morality, the soul's desire, to show its grateful love to the God who had redeemed it, and a new stimulus, in the belief that Christ and His Spirit work in the humblest individual Christian and that he enjoys intimate personal communion with God." [8]

With the passage of time, instruction became increasingly detailed and formalized out of the determination to maintain the unity of the Spirit and the bond of community. Thus the seeds of conformity were unwittingly nourished. Paradoxically, the development of Christianity brought its greatest danger, and its extension came hand in hand with its enemy. The establishment of the threefold ministry, the assignment of specific apostolic areas, the development of the catechumenate and other "administrative" divisions designed to implement and expedite the evangelistic and educational task of the church, were the raw materials of an unrealized and unwanted barrier between the individual and the recognition of a personal Savior. The lines of demarcation established to assist the church in its work served as well to render it ineffective. Under the demand for unity in its expanding efforts, the first wedge was driven into the principle of conversion by personal confrontation and commitment. It changed not only the direction but the concept of the church's educational ministry for centuries. This is especially evident in the areas of functional responsibility.

The teaching function in the church passed into the hands of an organized ministry, as did other responsibilities, although not always easily or gracefully. " But after the charismatic ministry was no longer in evidence . . . the church came to place its formal teaching, as well as its government, its administration of charity, and its priestly acts of worship, in the hands of its bishops, presbyters, and deacons." [9]

It was perhaps to be expected that the establishment of a rule to guide and maintain unity would, in time, become authoritarian. Such was, in fact, the historical progression that culminated in the various movements of reform and withdrawal. These movements were, for the most part, designed to restore the concept of responsible selfhood to its rightful place in the Christian community. Often, however, as is the case of the mystics, they took the form of retreat and isolation rather than redemption and community. Thus the full personalness of the New Testament experience gradually faded into the background to be replaced by a more generalized and methodical system of instruction, indoctrination, and administration. It was, however, never to be completely overcome or forgotten. " Jesus' precept that ' the kingdom of God is within you ' is the simple and clear expression of nonauthoritarian thinking. But only a few hundred years later, after Christianity had ceased to be only the religion of the poor and humble peasants, artisans, and slaves (the *Am haarez*) and had become the religion of those ruling the Roman Empire, the authoritarian trend in Christianity became dominant. Even so, the conflict between the authoritarian and humanistic principles in Christianity never ceased." [10]

The development of Christian education during the period

of the early and medieval church is paradoxical. On the one hand it sought to maintain the highly individualistic nature of Christian privilege and response. This was the purpose of the catechumenate and the need which drove the mystics " out " of the church. On the other hand, the church became so structured during this period of expansion and organization that the majority of persons had to increasingly rely on the symbolic interpretation of the basic formal acts of worship for such education as they received. The writings of this period of transition are reflective of the concern for the acknowledgment and development of the self.[11] They were, however, within either the intellectual or economic grasp of only a very few. The mass of men came to rely upon their spiritual leaders for such an interpretation of the pattern and purpose of the service of the child of God as they could hope to have. The boundaries of effective and affective action that so characterized the early New Testament communities of Christians had been increasingly narrowed. The end result was that by the Middle Ages the individual had become more of a canonical statistic than a contributing member of a dynamic fellowship.

The earlier Christian belief in the spiritual equality of men before God turned in the direction of a belief in a spiritual hierarchy. The necessities of these centuries being met as they were, the church, which was now also to say the Spirit, had come to speak through the bishops, singly or in councils, increasingly through a few members of the hierarchy competing for preeminence; and was preparing itself to speak through one man, a Pope. The will of God for man's common life came, it was believed, through just such channels. The Christian ethic was less and less a concern of love seeking how it might be expressed; more and more it was the church's fiat, the will of God heard through the clergy, growing specific in detail, sanctioned by the rewards of heaven and the pains of hell.[12]

This direction of growth and development clearly reflects the dual potential which the Christian church has had within itself from the beginning. It carries, on the one hand, a power of the Spirit that makes for the redemption and restoration of the human self. It also carries, on the other hand, in almost equal measure, a demonic power that threatens the basic concern for the self. This last is the power of separated man, and we must bear in mind that it is human creatures who in this world constitute the Christian community.[13]

This power of alienation and separation began to work its way in the historical development of the Christian church as it came out of its formative period of inspiration into the Middle Ages of interpretation and consolidation. In place of the free voice of the Spirit, there was established the authority of a norm as interpreted and enforced by both civil and ecclesiastical power. " The early conception of the church as a fellowship of believers, or the multitude of the faithful, or the society of Christians, was virtually lost in the middle ages except as it was kept alive in the ' heretical ' sects. Its place was increasingly taken by the notion of the church as a society of priests who alone are competent to perform the ecclesiastical acts and mediate between God and man." [14]

A similar development in the religious realm had occurred long before Christianity appeared on the earth, but from which the church, apparently, refused to learn. Israel had solidified around the hard core of the law and become a nation of code rather than a nation of response. Perhaps one of the reasons why the " new commandment " spoke with such clarity and appeal to men and women of the first century was its promise of release from such restrictive and irrelevant demands. The binding formality of a hard-and-fast code certainly provided men and women with no semblance of either recognition or an answer to their personal search or need. The reception accorded Christian truth was, in large measure, enervated by the sterility and irrelevance of such ecclesiastical formalism. Christianity's subsequent dereliction of its prime mission and concern was the greater tragedy precisely because the warmth and enthusiasm with which it had been received and which accounted for its growth was gradually being extinguished. That Christianity is not alone among the religions of the world in its failure to recognize this neither excuses it nor places it in a company of particular distinction.

> It is the tragedy of all great religions that they violate and pervert the very principles of freedom as soon as they become mass organizations governed by a religious bureaucracy. The religious organization and the men who represent it take over to some extent the place of family, tribe, and state. They keep man in bondage instead of leaving him free. It is no longer God who is worshiped but the group that claims to speak in his name. This has happened in all religions. Their founders guided man through the desert, away from the bondage of Egypt, while later on others have led him back toward a new Egypt though calling it the Promised Land.[15]

Thus it was that for the mass of men by the early medieval period, Christian truth had become a matter of symbol and, in many cases, superstition and routine practice. Under the severe and demanding rule of the hierarchy, the concepts and concerns of interpersonal confrontation and relationship between the individual and God virtually disappeared from view save in the treatise of the theologian or the reverie of the mystic. The evidence of this is found as the cause of one of the most powerful movements in the medieval church. "The history of scholastic thought is, in part, the story of human minds struggling by means of the weapons of dialectic to preserve the autonomy of the inner man in the midst of a world so largely dominated by the hierarchy."[16]

The period of expansion thus ended in a time and a process of solidification. The personal and immanent aspects of God's love for each and all of his individual children were neglected for the emphasis on his transcendence and the authority of his priesthood as the agency of his will. Conformity in thought, in word, and in action replaced the redemptive assurance of responsive and responsible people. Methodology and subservience replaced personal conversion and spiritual vitality during this significant period of the church's life and left a lasting imprint upon its educational role.

The Church presented itself to mankind, in varying degrees of thoroughness, as the controller of all human destiny here and hereafter. And this claim, though certainly not unchallenged, was accepted in Europe as a basis on which life must be ordered. This sovereignty of the Church, asserted, exercised, and as yet unbroken, makes of these eight hundred years a unity as far as education is concerned. For the Church undertook, not only to control a man's acts . . . , but still more, it undertook to control what he thought.[17]

## *Chapter Six*

# REACTION AND THE RISE OF HUMANISM

The educational, political, economic, and religious neglect of the individual, which reached its height during the medieval period, culminated in two great explosions that were similar in purpose although different in origin. The conformity that had been required of the mass of men was directed, in the main, by the desire of the few in authority to enforce their will as the standard of behavior and belief. Regardless of the intention and sincerity of the hierarchy, the individual of that time was caught up in the treadmill of a routine existence, with but little and infrequent opportunity to make his specific contribution to his art, his craft, his government, or his religion. The liege lord was supreme in all matters and " except for the monastic orders, which from time to time provided outlets for laymen discontented with silent docility, the masses of the baptized were relegated to the posture of spectators. In the medieval liturgy they never can adopt a more active role than adoration. " [1] Although there are great names of this period, they are, comparatively speaking, so few that they stand as a testimony to the fact of the subjection rather than the nurturing of selfhood in the lives of that particular time.

The humanistic reaction to this subjugation began with the Renaissance movement. Based on a high concept of the individual's uniqueness and the power of his reason, it utilized the resources of the age to develop the place of the individual within the social and philosophical order, particularly in the cultural and aesthetic sense. This attempt at the recovery or rediscovery of the primacy of the self was, in a sense, a protest against the neglect of the prime responsibility by the Christian church which had become for many an ecclesiastical sanction for civil action. By its apparent relation to the political order, its seeming concern for its temporal status and exchanged its commission to care for, nurture, and encourage security, the medieval church gave the impression of having the development of responsible selfhood for a pottage of cultural acceptance and security. The man of the Renaissance, violated and sensing his violation, struck back with the only power he had, the power of a self-based humanism.

If the medieval period can be considered, as has been suggested, as one of synthesis, then the Renaissance must be considered as a time of fragmentation, of separative activity. It sought to free the individual, to distinguish him as particular in the mass in which he had become lost, to offer him both release and energy for the expression of full selfhood in the several areas of thought and activity available, thereby breaking the constricting pattern and pressure of medieval life. It served as a catalyst and " initiated all those forces and tendencies in modern thought which either equated mind with self and derived virtue from reason, or which tried to understand the self in the context of some ontological framework." [2]

This humanistic movement had its counterpart in the Protestant Reformation, which was inspired, in part, by the ground swell of concern for the individual. It demonstrated a sensitivity to the violation of his rights in the religious as well as the political realm, and an awareness of the contradiction between the church's nurturing commission and its contemporary exercise of that responsibility.

Confronted by the physical and spiritual needs of the people of his time, the Augustinian monk Luther could not equate the activity of the church of his time with the pastoral and educational injunctions of its Lord. At the point of decision, he chose for the earlier pattern of activity and, professing allegiance to the foundation already laid rather than the practice of the contemporary church, he chose for individuality and directed all his efforts toward the reestablishment of that concept of selfhood which was from the beginning central in the educational ministry of the Christian community. Thus " the Reformation broke through the hard crust of authoritarianism by its assertion of the responsibility of the individual to exercise his private judgement." [3]

The actions of Luther and his followers violated the entrenched precepts of the church of the time on two counts. First, they challenged the arbitrary authority of the hierarchy on matters spiritual, and asserted the right and privilege of the individual to decision on the basis of personal encounter, conversion, and commitment. Second, they challenged the validity of a mysticism that sought to maintain individuality by means of an intense and thoroughgoing spirituality that tended to become a form of escape without practical cognizance of and concern for the welfare of one's neighbor in this present life. The Reformers pressed for the acknowledgment of distinct selfhood, the divinely expressed intention and desirability of individuality, and argued the necessity for a relevant and redemptive educational and pastoral involvement on the part of the church in all the affairs of human life. The courage of the Reformers is thus similar to and yet of a higher order than that of their secular contemporaries. " In the courage of the Reformers the courage to be as oneself is both affirmed and transcended. In comparison with the mystical form of courageous self-affirmation the Protestant courage of confidence affirms the individual self as an individual self in its encounter with God as person." [4]

The action of the Reformation was based on the revelation of the purpose of God as seen through his creative and redemptive activity, most notably in the incarnation and atonement. To bring light into darkness, to acquaint individuals with what God had done in his Christ, through his patriarchs and prophets, so they might see and hear, believe, repent and be saved, was the urgency behind the actions to translate the

Holy Scriptures and to provide catechetical instructions relevant to the level of concern and pointing toward the possibility of potential.

The purpose of God, by such means made known, spoke of sons rather than servants, of individuals rather than items. Thus the Reformers, operating from their understanding of divine intention, pressed toward the same goal as did the leaders of the Renaissance, who were motivated not so much by the revelation of divine intention as by the recognition of human need. The similarity of concern and purpose but difference of perspective and motive is perhaps most clearly to be seen in the respective reactions to the rule of the papacy. "The Reformation and the Renaissance also have different motives for objecting to Papal authority. The Reformation regards the clerical authoritarianism as an affront to the majesty of God, while the Renaissance regards it as a threat to the liberty of the mind." [5]

In the Reformation movement, the greatest disappointment came when, in the search for individuality and the free expression of responsible selfhood, a new authoritarianism threatened to replace the old. The discipline of "The Book," interpreted as an ironbound rule for the conduct of life and binding on the body politic, became as demanding, subjugating, and conformity-ridden as the very structure against which it had protested. It was able to develop and maintain itself more by a stubborn strength of resistance to persecution than by an indwelling of the power of the Spirit of God. With but few exceptions, the fanaticism of the Reformers and their followers resulted in a new threat to genuine, purposive, and expressive individual selfhood under God. Once more it was "repeatedly made clear that the common folk were to stay in their stations and leave religious matters to those professionally trained to handle them. The 'priesthood of all believers' became, therefore, the lay priesthood of Christian princes and town councillors advised by theologians and canon lawyers." [6]

It is small wonder, then, that although communities of the

Reformers grew and for a time flourished at various spots around the globe, the dearth of their personal warmth served to reveal the inconsistency of their new legalism in the light of the love and freedom proffered and promised by Jesus the Christ as the fruit of the new community. Thus it was that soon in the order of time individuals began to free themselves from the chains of this new demand, continuing to search for the freedom they had been promised, for which they had been created, but which they had not yet experienced.[7]

It may well be that the failure of the Reformation to remain true to the principles of the original concern, the rigidity of its political and ecclesiastical discipline, the pre-Christian legalism of its social and moral code, all served to feed and foster the impulse to humanism on the part of the leaders of the Renaissance movement. It is certainly true that " the glorious liberty of the children of God " was little more in evidence in Geneva or the Massachusetts Bay Colony of the seventeenth century than it was in Spain or France in the sixteenth.

In the continuing search for inner freedom, for self-understanding, for self-realization, man was once again forced to turn to himself for what he could discover and determine. In the quest for the comprehension and realization of such dignity and meaning as he might have, the individual began to build his philosophy, his science, and his religion on the basis of what he saw and heard and knew as empirically true. At the center of the new system was man, not God. The man of the Renaissance was bold with the boldness of desperation. He was adventurous with the adventurousness of one who saw that he had little to lose and almost everything to gain.[8]

Derelict though the church may have been, and desirable as the goal of self-attained individuality might appear, the fact remains that both the means and the frame of reference of the humanist were in error. Man cannot find, establish, and maintain himself out of relationship to the One who gave him life and the promise of an everlasting selfhood. The attempt at a secular-based concept of selfhood, developed in reaction to the conformity of the medieval period, was in effect based upon the false premise of autonomy. It could not help resulting in moral and intellectual anarchy. The tragedy lay in the fact that after generations of too little, man in seeking for his selfhood endangered himself by the threat of too much.

To ascribe final worth to persons is in effect to deny Christianity's claim that man is a contingent creature. The secular humanist may legitimately attribute final or absolute value to persons; for to him there is no being beyond man himself. Christian faith, however, cannot do this without sacrificing an essential element in its doctrine of man. For it is the Christian faith that man is a theonomous being. This means that man is not autonomous or final, but derives his meaning and value from his relation to God, the highest value. When, therefore, the principle of respect for personality is carried to the length of endowing persons with supreme worth, then the Christian conception of human value is perverted. The way is then opened for a subtle deification of humanity. And this, in turn, starts a trend toward the kingdom of man as a substitute for the Kingdom of God.[9]

This is precisely what occurred in the centuries following what may be considered as the spiritual failure of the Protestant Reformation to remain true to its fundamental Biblical principles and to incorporate them into the daily round of the community life. Throughout the period there were the small voices upholding the right of the individual to nurture, asserting the privilege of personal consideration and the inestimable value of personal commitment. Such men as Pestalozzi, Froebel, and, in a later time but nonetheless a kindred spirit, Bushnell, were the victims of the pressure to conform. Despite the pressures of both tradition and novelty, despite the attacks of both the hierarchy and their contemporaries, these men and a few like them remained true to the ideal of responsible selfhood as revealed by God in Christ. They saw this as the solemn " developmental task " of every Christian community at every level of its life.

With the warm insights of a faithful few subject to such attacks, and an increasing firmness on the part of the established hierarchy, it should come as no surprise that the individual became caught up in the daring challenge and found himself uplifted by the emotional appeal of secular humanism in "The Age of Reason." For many, rationalism became a religion substitute, not so much on its own merits as by the absence of any virile alternative. The power of the human mind was acknowledged and accepted as the greatest motivating force in the world. The major contributions to human thought and development during the next three hundred years following the Protestant Reformation were made by secularism or deism. Out of these increasingly strong movements came many of the social principles of individual freedom and dignity which were of the essence of the Christian gospel, but without its firm foundation of responsive and reconciling love. Reason ruled, and to reason was given both the glory and the homage. The church existed, but lacked the vitality and the courage of its Lord to mingle, to confront, to convert, to be in and yet not of the world.

During this significant span of time Christian truth was seldom presented as relevant to the cultural enterprise and even less frequently as capable of redemptive action therein. More often than not it was both presented and pictured as an irrelevant force of opposition to any and all forms and possibilities of change. The clerical caricature that appears in the Victorian novel is a sophisticated commentary on the end result in the minds of the laity. An external estimate of the church's witness found it for the most part critical rather than constructive and, when finally aroused from the somnolence inspired by its traditional security, ultraconservative to the point of a reactionary negativism. To the eyes of man the Christian community at any given time and place appeared to be primarily concerned with its own perpetuation rather than with its responsibility to illuminate and lead those in darkness and confusion. Membership was a matter of custom and convenience rather than the result of confrontation, conversion, and commitment.

For a time the forces of humanism disregarded the church even as it had disregarded its obligation to them and all the sheep committed to its care. By the late nineteenth century, however, the revolt of the individual against all that held him in and down arrived and knocked at the gate of the Christian church. The irrelevance of the church's preaching and teaching in the light of the problems of the day, the issues of the time, was attacked from both within and without the community. Once again, the church itself became the locus and focus of re-formation. This is nowhere more apparent than in the philosophy of Christian education. Under the dominance of a scientifically oriented culture, and spurred by the demands of a reason-worshiping laity, the historic theology of the church began to be interpreted from and in the light of the existential situation. The historic relevance of the will of God for the way of man was discovered anew. The discovery, however, was attributed to the intelligence of man rather than the grace of God, and the order of priority gave precedence to the desires of men rather than the declarations of God.[10]

The concept of sin was filed by title, and the humanity of Jesus was stressed with a fervor not seen since the time of Pelagius. Man was presented not so much as a child of God as he was a valuable partner without whom God could not succeed. Mortal man was liberating theology from the restricting shackles that made it difficult to comprehend, and the Biblical doctrine of sin did not allow man appropriate grandeur for the enterprise. Instead of rewriting the doctrine of sin, the new or " liberal " theologians chose to bypass and obscure the nature and fact of sin as recognized and defined by centuries of the Judeo-Christian tradition, and " never adequately expressed the depth of our dependence on the redemptive work of God." [11]

The essence of the movement was analyzed with both clarity and accuracy by T. O. Wedel, writing from the vantage point of historical perspective:

Heaven has become the realm of human ideals, the goal of human aspiration. Hell has been transmuted into immortality. The old wine of biblical imagery is thus poured into new bottles; and both Bible and traditional Christian dogma is, indeed, honored on formal occasions as of old, and their hallowed vocabulary and imagery utilized in preaching. But the change that has taken place, when properly understood, is, nevertheless, momentous. For the Bible has, in reality, been reduced to the story of religious man and his climb upward toward Deity; it has ceased to be the story of God Himself, speaking in the Law and through the Prophets, and Himself invading man's world as "Word made Flesh." [12]

Educationally speaking, one of the most significant developments of the early twentieth century was the philosophy of John Dewey and his disciples. Progressive education, as it came to be known in the popular parlance, was a natural partner of the cultural trend, and its adoption by large portions of the Christian church's educational system was a logical result of the secular redemption of Christianity. This adoption did not, however, serve to implement the primary nurturing function of the church as much as it served to reveal the instability of the church's sense of mission and purpose. It clearly indicated the church's awareness and eagerness to be included on the educational bandwagon, and pointed up the church's failure to religiously and realistically contribute to the needs of its people on the basis of the pattern and the purpose revealed by God in Christ.

In one sense, progressive religious education represented the placing of a thin veil of sanctity over and around a concern that was fundamentally secular and humanistic. "The idea . . . is rooted in the assumption that religious experience emerges where self-realizing persons creatively adjust themselves to their natural and social world. On this basis the creative center is located in self-striving man, who is conceived as the builder of the Kingdom." [13] There were, of course, many who saw through the veil and recognized the danger and the defection implicit in this movement. The trend met with both argument and strong conflict, but its opponents did not stand on common ground. There were many and they were vocal in the expression of their desire to have the church remain apart and unsullied from the world. The difficulty, the conflict, arose because the church had done precisely that. The pendulum was on the move, and critics of the church's educational reconstruction were accused of obscurantism, conservatism, and a stubborn unwillingness to accept a new revelation for a new age. Neither critics nor proponents, nor even those who found themselves somewhere between the lines fast being drawn, had the option or the moratorium on truth. Who, for example, could deny either the correctness or the concern expressed in the following manner by one of the " liberals "?

The social process of religious education, which critics of religious education hold dear because they think it is centered too much in human life, is the very process which gives the largest promise of bringing about a vital experience of God. Vitality of religious experience is not realized by turning away from the problems and decisions of human life in efforts to find a direct relationship to God. It is only as individuals and groups are engaged in the enterprise of God on earth that they can truly find a relationship to him. Bible study and prayer and worship will not of themselves produce vital religious experience. It is only when these are utilized because of a concern for human life and because of a sense of need for resources beyond those which seem available to human endeavor that they lead to the vitalizing of the religious experience. The experience of God is integrally related to a social process of religious education.[14]

No argument or debate conducted on the basis of intelligent conviction and sincerity is pointless. But the point that is finally proved is not always the one advanced by either party to the debate. So it was in the case of the religious education controversy that reached its high point during the second and third decades of the twentieth century. It illustrated beyond question the basic weakness of the church, the ineffectiveness that had plagued it since the late apostolic period and that accounted for its dereliction and deficiencies. Basically, the weakness is a concern for methodology rather than individuality, a preoccupation with systematized security on the world's terms rather than significant service in the search for selfhood on the Lord's terms.

The various contributions to the philosophy of Christian education through the years each brought with it both merit and truth. None of them either began or intended to be a limited or extremist point of view. Too often, however, guided by the will and the pride of man rather than the Spirit and the revelation of God, each failed and fell short of the contribution that it could have made to the individual and to the community of which he was a part. In the case of the liberal movement there was a mistaken sacrifice of the power of God for the sense of the immediacy of his presence. It resulted from an unwitting incorporation of secular political philosophy into a realm that by definition transcends such a system but which, by the blindness and vanity of man, was allowed to assume a position of control. "As over against a concept of God as one who stands aloof from the human struggle, who rules by arbitrary decree, and who manipulates persons as mechanical puppets, the democratic idea of God is certainly to be preferred. But insofar as the democratic idea of God obscures the fact that God is wholly sovereign in His Kingdom, and that man is utterly dependent upon God, it must be regarded as defective." [15]

The contribution of liberalism was its awareness that the church is the society of which all men are members by virtue of divine intention and human potential. It is not a self-contained, self-perpetuating group that merely lays down requirements for those who seek membership. Qualifications for membership are not defined in terms of dotted *i*'s and crossed *t*'s. Contrary to other human organizations, "candidates" for membership come out of weakness and unacceptability more than out of strength and acceptability. The church not only recognizes the needs and tensions of the time in which it finds itself in history; it takes those needs and tensions to itself and contains them within its own body. Its task and its trust is to be so alert to the insights and contributions of the historical era, both positive and negative, that these can be recognized, interpreted, and illuminated in the light of the eternal love and purpose of God for his children and his creation. Thus not only the assumptions springing from faith assurance but the critical judgments resulting from intelligent recognition are blended into a lasting harmony for the benefit of the individual and the community that contributes to him and derives from him. The concern for the individual, for the self, was at the core of the liberal movement. It did not seek " to train the reason and to develop the intelligence in order to curb egoistic desires and strengthen social impulses " but " to utilize the intelligence in organizing the life of the family, the school, and the church, and indeed the larger group relationships of industry, nation and internal relations, increasingly on a truly corporate basis." [16]

It is a truism to say that the needs of the twentieth century demanded a new perspective. The relic of Victorian Christian education was no more suitable to the dynamics of the post World War I era than any other Victorian relic. The advances of science and technology were so rapid and so significant that the individual found himself in danger of becoming a not-always-necessary adjunct to the machine age. For many, Huxley's *Brave New World* was not so much science fiction as it was a serious and significant prophecy of things to come. Paradoxically, however, the developments that promised liberation led to the very brink of moral, social, and economic enslavement. Once again the wheel had turned too far. " The individualism of the liberal society was prompted by a moral error; and the technical developments of modern civilization served to support the error. The moral error was the notion that individuals could be self-justifying ends." [17]

During the several hundred years of this period, the failure of the Christian church to be concerned for the individual as an entity, and to speak and minister relevantly to his or her particular needs and fears, caused the individual to seek elsewhere for the definition and possible fulfillment of selfhood. Forced back on himself, the individual found his perspective increasingly limited and his possibility of successful seeking similarly frustrated. As D. C. Wyckoff has pointed out: " To avoid a Christian perspective leads on the one hand to the substitution of secular religious values, whose fate is to stand outside the door of Biblical faith yearning for what lies within but unwilling to enter. Or it leads, on the other hand, to limitation of aim and even to bitterness and cynicism." [18]

The liberal school must be commended for its zeal in attempting to overcome the church's weak concern and virtual disregard of the individual during the preceding generations. The commendation is all the more deserved because of the hostility with which the message of the liberals was greeted because of the disregard of the individual as experienced by him. One cannot, however, excuse the fact that instead of presenting the clear portrayal of kerygmatic truth, the liberals appeared to operate and attempt to convert from the ground on which man stood rather than the truth of which God spoke. In the desire to gain a hearing, the tendency was to simplify the gospel, to make it more appealing to and in accord with the limited understanding of the individual of the time. The presentation was made on the basis of the common denominator as seen in the outward signs rather than in a deepening awareness of and sensitivity to the challenging and penetrating presence of God. As had happened in times past, so in this age, it was only this vital confrontation which called forth from man the full response of his selfhood at its deepest and most meaningful level. The tendency to equate God's will with man's way offered Christian education the opportunity to speak with vigor and clarity to man of his priority in the order of creation and of his prime responsibility in the family of God. The need was imperative and the opportunity was at hand to make the vital distinction between the understanding of man and the intention of God.

Against this tendency to obscure the distinction between the Kingdom of God and any given social order, Christian nurture is forced to protest if it is to serve as a vital agency of faith in the Church of tomorrow. It must recognize that the Kingdom of which Jesus spoke will always be a transcendent reality never to be fully translated into the relative forms of human culture. Christian faith must therefore sharply protest any tendency to equate the Kingdom of God with democracy or with any other type of social order.[19]

The unwillingness of the church of this period to make this distinction and to define itself as separate from, yet involved in, the world of its witness, resulted in a laissez-faire type of conversion and resultant qualities of membership. The church tended to become one agency among many, instead of the locus of inspiration and illumination. It became, in short, competitive rather than redemptive, concerned more for its acceptance by others than its responsible and reconciliatory acceptance of them. Such neglect or betrayal of stewardship led many to choose for the honesty of agnosticism or the courage of secular humanism. The right to such a choice was based on the premise that " a God about whose existence or non-existence you can argue is a thing beside others within the universe of existing things." [20] Under the loose interpretation of liberal humanism, the individual could choose for or against God with perfect impunity, for man's freedom was expostulated and emphasized to the neglect of his responsibility. This delusion was shaken only by the incontrovertible evidence of fascism, nazism, and communism. The development and destructive swath of these idolatries was unwittingly fostered by Christian neglect and the dereliction of both individual and corporate Christian responsibility.

The regrettable alienation of modern culture from Christianity must be understood, in part, as a reaction against ecclesiastical shackles which, if they had not been thrown off, really would have prevented man from carrying through important forms of progress, enlightenment and self-understanding. The failure of Christianity to furnish an organic center for culture has meant that many of these potentially creative powers have run riot. Modern society, armed with technology and dreaming of self-sufficiency, has been set adrift to fashion its own gods and ideologies. These dreams have indeed brought our civilization to the edge of the abyss.[21]

# III

# RESOURCES, RESISTANCE, AND RESOLUTION

*These things I have spoken unto you, that in me ye might have peace. In the world ye shall have tribulation: but be of good cheer; I have overcome the world.* — John 16:33.

*Chapter Seven*

# RESOURCES FOR RESPONSE

Both the church and the individual bear the responsibility for the proper understanding and positive utilization of the resources available for the achievement of selfhood. The fullness of selfhood cannot be comprehended or communicated apart from the totality of influence exerted upon it and issuing from both this and the larger life. The exercise of selfhood is restricted unless and until it is allowed the full expression of its various components in response to the desires within and the demands from without. " As the Christian attaches himself to his God, to his church, and relates himself to this world, he finds in this engagement his own selfhood. . . . Because God is personal he forces man into a dialogue, and calls man to his true selfhood in freedom, in service, and in his church." [1]

The individual who has become alive to his potential for selfhood and the possibility of its achievement will not settle for that which speaks or ministers to only a part of his need. The desire of man for wholeness becomes demand as he approaches the portal of possibility. Thus the Christian community must recognize and present a context sufficiently broad and deep to nurture the self in both its individual and corporate endeavors. A comprehensive realism is both implicit and imperative in the church's nurturing activity. H. S. Elliott cautioned recognition of this fact when he wrote: " The churches have to face the modern world and it would be inadvisable for them to attempt to develop program and methodology as if there had been no contributions from education, psychology, mental hygiene, sociology, and other similar work. Therefore, a philosophy of religious education should offer a way for adjusting these two points of emphasis." [2]

The historical survey of Part II illustrates the pendulum action of the church's nurturing philosophy and practice. Out of this background and the apparent contemporary reaction to it certain conclusions are evident.

> Claiming that orthodoxy had forfeited its claim upon modern man by its failure to update Christianity and that no man could any longer be orthodox and intellectually honest, liberalism accommodated Christianity to what it regarded as the demands of modern scholarship. It was therefore ironical that history itself arose to discredit liberalism by demonstrating that the actual world was quite different from the one to which liberalism had adjusted. History itself undid liberalism's faith in its character and inevitable progress. In the deep crisis of the twentieth century there appeared a depravity and demonic brutality which demonstrated that liberalism's morally intact man ever moving toward perfection was non-existent. Although an estimate of the human situation has rarely been more mistaken, liberalism would still be very much alive had it been challenged merely by orthodoxy. It has, however, been challenged and discredited by history itself.[3]

In view of this historical sweep and involvement, Christian education must be particularly sensitive to and of the secular philosophies and pressures exerted upon the individual. The temporal conditions under which the individual lives, the demands he faces, the opportunities that confront him, the challenges that threaten him, the creative intention of God — all these are the raw materials out of which he constructs the purpose of his life. " The Christian need not settle for an education that is partly secular and partly Christian, for if education actually involves seeing things as they are and coming to grips with life, it can hardly be complete unless carried on within a fully Christian perspective." [4]

Only as these are brought together, when the eternal comes

in to grasp the temporal, is there the possibility of such relevance as is the solid food of the redemptive process. The statement of Randolph Crump Miller can serve as a beacon: "When theology is meaningful and related to life, it is possible to make use of the experiences of all of life to build a Christian perspective in the light of the learner's situation and age-group, illuminating those experiences with the peculiarly Christian experiences of worship, sacrament, preaching, study, fellowship, and work as found within the life of the Church." [5]

The degree to which Christian education is aware of and involved in the daily affairs and concerns of human life is the degree to which the individual has the possibility of recognizing his selfhood under God. Only as Christianity is cognizant of and on speaking terms with the human situation can the perspective and purpose of its educational function be recognized and received. Redemption is wrought in the midst of life. "It is only in the integral relationship of the individual and the social that a realistic religious education can be developed." [6] Therefore, we turn now to a brief survey of a few of the major areas of resource in and by which the individual is encouraged and informed to respond to the desire for self-appreciation and self-fulfillment under God.

The first of these is Biblical theology. The wisdom of Holy Scripture is a treasury of the will of God at work in this world. By a relevant presentation of it there is a conjoining of the nature and the need of man as he defines it and as it is defined by the creative God. It is a historical book and speaks to the present participants in the drama. It "speaks out of the immediate and concrete realities of history, where men doubted and believed, hated and loved, despaired and hoped. Its message comes from the depth of life and speaks to the depth within us. . . . Therefore it is understandable that as modern people wrestle with the issues of destiny in their own contemporary situation, they often find themselves in rapport with the prophets and apostles of the Bible." [7]

As a resource for the communication and responsible development of selfhood, the use of the Bible in Christian education should far exceed the normative round of content by title, the magic of Old Testament "hero" stories, or a short course in geography based on the missionary journeys of Paul. Fundamentally, the Bible is the story of individuals who perceived and accepted or rejected the reality of God as evidence in their lives and their world. The cardinal point of Biblical theology as recital, however, is that as it has been in the past, so will it continue to be in the present and the future. The element of identification by the reader with the participant is emphasized. Thus we may say that "the central purpose of using the Bible in Christian education is *to prepare the way for men to perceive God and respond to him in the present*." [8]

This dynamic concept of Biblical theology reveals not only the paucity of the concern for the communication of static content, but it points up the need for personal involvement and the benefits thereof. James D. Smart, for one, challenges us to recognize the validity of this point:

> The aim of our teaching must reach far beyond the transmitting of information about the Bible and its contents. We are training children, young people, and adults to be witnessing disciples in a non-Christian world. The power of their witness will be . . . to act and speak in accordance with the faith and life that are manifest in the Bible and that become theirs through the word of the Bible.[9]

It is the personal aspect of Bible study that illuminates and inspires responsible selfhood in any age. As the recorded events testify to a personal relationship between God and his children in the past, the reading individual of the present is moved to participate in a similar endeavor of personal search and encounter. In the words of G. Ernest Wright, "by means of historical memory and identification he participates, so to speak, in the original events. Then, facing his own situation he confesses his faith and his sin, he seeks God's forgiveness and direction." [10]

This dynamic of individual encounter, recognition, and response leads to the development of genuine community when shared with others of similar experience. The sense of the immanent presence of God becomes as much a reality in the life of modern man as it was, for example, to Abraham, who responded to a vocation he did not choose or comprehend. The concept of Biblical theology as recital gives a perspective that is in sharp contrast to the objective and sophisticated type of religious instruction so customary and so sterile for our time. The disparity between these two is defined by Bernhard Anderson:

The men of the Bible do not tell us about grasping principles or propositions; they tell us about being grasped by God himself in the midst of crucial events of their history. They do not tell us about their knowing God as an object of reflective thought; rather, they tell us about being *known by* God down at the "grass roots" level of their existence where they faced the immediate issues of daily life.[11]

Thus "the frame of meaning established by Biblical faith is able to give meaning to both the individual and the collective dramas of history."[12] To communicate both the validity and the vitality of this is the prime function of Christian education. The realization of this nurturing responsibility is particularly significant in these days of mounting delinquency, the increasing number of school dropouts, and the obvious deterioration of sound moral standards. We can neither present these young people with, nor expect them to find, Christian solutions to contemporary problems "unless, in the midst of them, they begin to hear what God has to say to them, and they can find no interest in the Bible until they discover that the word it speaks has to do with the very problems that are most urgent for them."[13]

Biblical theology speaks of the verification of God's historical action to and for the benefit of the individual. Presented in the light and knowledge of man's existential frustration and despair, Biblical theology presents the full and acceptable expression of man's individuality as the basis for the genuine community that is in accord with the purpose of God and that for which man was created. The balance between immediacy and ultimacy so necessary to the well-being of the individual is presented in the Bible as the firm ground for which the individual seeks and upon which he can stand.

We are confronted with evidence that the thesis of Biblical faith, that the self is in dialogue with a God who must be defined as a " person " because he embodies both the structure of being and transcendent freedom, is more valid than the alternative theses which find much greater favor among the sophisticated. The Biblical thesis requires a more explicit act of faith because it leaps a gap of discontinuity between man and God and because it dares to give a specific meaning to the divine, which is relevant to the partial and fragmentary meanings of history. It both fulfills and corrects these meanings, loyalties and values, and therefore has a more valid attitude and a transcendent self's historical existence which the various rationalistic systems affirm too simply and the mystic thesis annuls too absolutely.[14]

Secondly, among the resources available to Christian education and to the individual for the nurture and development of the self is the field of research and study broadly comprehended under the title of " Psychiatry." By virtue of a mutual concern for the individual, the relationship between religion and psychiatry is close. The fundamental distinction between the church's concern and psychiatric insight is found in the frame of reference. The church ministers out of an ultimate context of continuing growth in both this life and the next. Psychiatry functions in the immediate realm, with a concern for humanistic acceptance and adjustment. Each can make a contribution to the other. The individual benefits from the relevant combination of methodology and perspective.

Randolph Crump Miller has made the point that Christian opposition to or neglect of psychiatric insight has, in the past, been injurious to both the church and the individual. He suggests that the resolution of the difficulty is the responsibility of Christian education insofar as it can and should use whatever means are available to interpret human experience. " The new task is to make theology relevant, realizing . . . that truth may be acquired only through the interpretation of experience, and that we become Christians only as we use truth to place ourselves in commitment to the living God revealed to us in Jesus Christ and through the fellowship of the Church." [15]

The insights of psychiatry are of such a nature and extent that its reports and evaluations can be of great assistance to Christians as the church attempts to minister to the needs of the individual, speaking to him in understandable terms, relevant to the particular situation. Oftentimes these needs are subdued or disguised. Unless and until they are recognized and accepted for themselves in the fullness of their reality, in the starkness of their actuality, by both the individual and the church, there can be no relevant and redemptive ministry and certainly no effective, constructive nurture.

The relationship between religion and psychotherapy is reciprocal. In particular, " psychotherapy has demonstrated an effectiveness of method and a validity of principle from which representatives of religon and their people can greatly profit." [16] On the other hand, we can see that " for mental health men need two things from religion: knowledge of God's mighty and eternal love for them, and opportunity to respond personally to that love with all they have." [17]

The ability and willingness of the individual to recognize and accept reality is an essential element in Christian education and nurture. The individual must be enabled to see and encouraged to be the fullness of himself, in both his actuality and his potentiality. He must be helped to accept the fact that he is of value in and of himself, irrespective of his cultural status or contribution. Such unacceptability as he may count a barrier is a fact of need rather than a ground for rejection in the pastoral eyes of the church. The freedom to be and to express himself that the individual experiences in the psychoanalytic experience can and should be known even more clearly and comfortingly within the Christian community. One of the prime contributions psychiatry may have to make to Christian education is the principle and the practice of acceptance. " It provides a situation in which a person can be completely honest with himself and with a fellow human being. Conversely, it provides a situation in which he can discover how much he has deceived himself hitherto; the manner in which his ideal picture of himself, his unrecognized needs, and his special way of trying to make the universe conform to his private demands, have caused him to distort reality." [18]

Psychiatry, then, as a resource for Christian education, can define the dilemma in depth on the basis of what might be termed its " acceptive attentiveness " to the needs of the individual. Its reports and estimates can be of great significance for and assistance to the nurturing work of the church.

Psychotherapy has pointed out that man needs nothing so much as relief from the sense of isolation, or estrangement. The Church believes in a God who, far from holding himself aloof from sinful man, comes into the very midst of human life for the express purpose of effecting man's salvation. The good news of the Church, then, is that God wills to effect a reconciliation of man with Himself obviously not on the questionable basis of man's uneven conformity but on the certain basis of His own everlasting love for a creature who never really conforms. Indeed, this God is not looking for conformity but for fellowship; what He wills is that man respond to Him with whatever he has. In one way and another, all forms of the Christian religion believe these things. What is needed, therefore, is the fuller appreciation of their implications in the varied ministration of the Church.[19]

Thirdly, as a resource there is the expressive element of worship, an outgrowth and acknowledgment of the content and concern made apparent in each and both of the two previous areas, and an opportunity for both recognition and response. As one discovers and identifies one's self as participant in the Biblical drama and admits the depth of desire and need brought to the distinguishable service by the various forms and techniques of psychotherapy, there is found in the worshiping action a possibility for expression that unites the various strands of life.

Charles Stinnette asserts that " worship reveals the ultimate commitments of a man's life. It is expressed in the offering of himself. . . . Worship is sacrifice and oblation; it is losing one's self and finding one's self in relation to the source of existence." [20] Thus for both Christian education and the searching individual, the recognition of the resource available for expression in both particularity and concert is comprehensively constructive. In the act of worship, be it personal or corporate, there is opportunity to bring one's self into relationship with that which gives meaning to the experience. The worshiping experience provides the individual with the occasion to bring into relationship the eternal and the temporal dimensions of his life, so that each may be informed by the other, and both may be conjoined to contribute to the meaningfulness of the human pursuit.

Randolph Crump Miller calls worship " life-centered education at its best, for in the worship of the Church the learner is in the presence of God, and thus there is the opportunity for the development of faith and the receiving of grace." [21] This becomes increasingly apparent as one participates, for at the same time the dimension of transcendent possibility is introduced. For both the individual and the faithful community the act of worship implicitly involves them in an assertion of the self-transcendent possibility. Participation with the historical contemporaries is informed and enlightened by the faithful knowledge that this participation is in the long train of historical participation, and that they, each and all, are involved with an eternal progression of purpose in the worshiping act, which expresses the existential concern and the external commission.

Fourthly, there is the resource of personal prayer and meditation. Informed by the understanding revealed in Biblical theology, goaded by the need acknowledged through psychoanalysis and psychoanalytic insight, and encouraged by participation in the worshiping community, the individual acknowledges and seeks to reinforce the possibility of responsible selfhood under God through personal prayer and meditation. It has been said that prayer is personal but never private. The validity of this is quite apparent in the community structure wherein self-recognition and self-fulfillment are live possibilities.

The practice of prayer takes many forms — praise, thanksgiving, adoration, intercession, petition, and perhaps most important and certainly most neglected, listening. All too often there is a reversal of the proper role of the servant as seen in the call of Samuel. Where he replied to the voice of God by saying, "Speak, Lord, for thy servant hears," many a modern demands, "Hear, Lord, for thy servant speaks!" No matter how personal our prayer, it stems from and flows back into the human context in which we live. Thus our acknowledgments of God's glory and our own shortcomings involve others and bring them within the scope and context of God's love for the individual and the individual's desire for God.

As Reuel Howe suggests, "Prayer is an act of love; it is choosing to meet God and man and to live in mutual relation with them. . . . Prayer is the practice of our new relationship for the sake of all men who are killing themselves and each other for want of Him who would receive them unto Himself." [22]

Whether our prayer is personal or corporate or a blend of both, as is the more usual pattern, it is a response to the encounter and an expression of it in which the self presents itself before God in thanksgiving for recognition, in penitence for failure, and in faith for further striving.[23] The regular practice may begin as a discipline, but it culminates in the joy of an anticipated reunion. As one withdraws into a figurative closet for meditation upon the production of the day or the week, one is confronted with the promise of him who said, "Come unto me, all ye that travail and are heavy laden, and I will refresh you." In this meeting there is consideration, confession, consolation, and comfort that enable a return to the world and an increasingly significant response to God and the human community.

Prayer arises in men's hearts because men need God. It arises as the response of men to the God in whom they live and move and have their being. Men pray because they cannot help it. They praise and adore him with their prayers, they grovel and writhe in the agony of their sins, they lift up their faces in repentance and confession, and their faces light up with the assurance of faith that absolution is theirs; they ask for what they truly desire for themselves and for others, and they receive the blessing of God's forgiving and power-giving grace.[24]

It would not be unfair to surmise that the greatest activity which passes for prayer in the busy world of today takes place in moments of crisis. It is not so much an acknowledgment as it is a Mayday signal of distress to any who may be tuned in. Although credit may be given to the instinctive action of the so-called arrow prayer, cognizance must also be taken of the fact that it is contrary to, and out of context with, the consistent pattern of the individual life. Gordon Allport reminds us that " a foxhole is a poor place in which to learn to pray, for the religion of a merely frightened man is likely to evaporate as soon as the danger is removed." [25] Foxholes are not limited to battlefields, and the concern of Christian education to nurture a realistic relationship between the Creator and his children that will be prior to the foxholes of life and subsequent to the existential crises is based on conviction rather than chaos. Granted the fact of calamity in human life, Christian nurture is concerned for both prologue and epilogue to the crisis as it seeks to develop within the individual the true sense of selfhood in relation to God, against which the very gates of hell cannot prevail.

Presentation, therefore, and practice of the resource of prayer and meditation, both personal and corporate, contributes to the individual's understanding of the nature of responsible selfhood under God. It fosters and is, in return, fostered by community expressions of and responses to the place of the self in the purpose of God.

A fifth area of resource for the development of self-understanding and self-fulfillment in the providence of God is the area of the sacramental life. Although there are different degrees of emphasis on sacramental theology, in the main, within the Christian tradition, there is agreement that there are such vehicles of communication, and that whether they be two or seven, they are, educationally speaking, valuable focuses for the understanding and acceptance of God's continuing presence and action in human history.

For the shortness of our vision and the hardness of our hearts, certain instrumentalities have been chosen to represent that which, by its very nature, is unrepresentable. In and of themselves "the outward and visible signs" are not "holy." They are sanctified by and in their use as channels of grace and tangible evidences of our hope of glory. The gift of God to the individual in the person of Jesus Christ becomes immediate as the individual recalls "the night in which he was betrayed," and partakes in grateful humility of that spiritual nourishment designated as a remembrance of his sacrifice "for the sins of the whole world." There is no magic here, save as the sacrament is divorced from the saving action accomplished once in time for all time. There is, rather, a reality of recollection and a reality of response as once again the individual becomes aware that God has come into the human realm in order that the individual may live and have life more abundantly than in his isolation, apart from God, his love and his purpose.

As Biblical theology is recital and elicits identification and response, so do the sacraments dramatize the high points of Christian selfhood under God and encourage affirmation and acceptance. These are aids for our limited understanding and our feeble steps, designed to strengthen and encourage by reminder and refreshment the forgetful and hungry soul.

Christian education has many forms and a variety of teaching devices. Each of the previously mentioned areas represents both a possibility and a means for the realistic and beneficial nurture of the self. In the words of Paul: "Everything created by God is good, and nothing is to be rejected if it is received with thanksgiving." (I Tim. 4:4.) As the self is dynamic, so is education and nurture of any relevant sort, and Christian education and pastoral care must make use of all the resources available and recognizable if it is to benefit the individual.

Christian education is not the province of specialists any more than its proper exercise is restricted to a particular place or time of the week. The local church, the home, the committed individual, the incidents of human glory and tragedy, are all participants in the effective nurture of the self. The primary challenge to Christian education today is that if the faith is to have relevance " for a twentieth century mind trained to think in twentieth century terms and pre-supposing a twentieth century reference, we must face a tremendous task of reinterpretation of the faith in terms and figures which have meaning to such a mind." [26]

One of the most effective devices for such interpretation and expression is found in the educational technique of the study and discussion group. There is no assurance of success in numbers, be they large or small. Experience has shown, however, in classes for all ages, that opportunity to participate in group teaching and inquiry affords an opportunity to listen to, react for or against, question, and " internalize " relevant content as communicated in a highly personal context. In the small-group situation, the place and contribution of the individual is emphasized. In the protective fellowship of concern, the self is able to comprehend that just as agreement does not guarantee acceptance, neither does disagreement end in exclusion.

As Elton Trueblood has suggested, " The crucial question today is not whether we must have a fellowship . . . ; the crucial question concerns the *character* of the fellowship. The more we think about it the more we realize that it must be a fellowship of the committed." [27] Trueblood, of course, is speaking here of the end result, but the truth applies as well to the beginnings of such a fellowship, however weak and ill-defined they may be. The constitution of a study and discussion group usually represents an element of commitment; commitment to a concern, commitment to the search for understanding, if not to the accomplishment of it.

The contemporary study and discussion group usually proceeds out of an awareness of the existential situation and is concerned to refer to that common experience as the testing ground, the illustrating ground, of much that is considered by the group and the individual who comprise it. An intelligent and clear analysis of the present or sound survey of the past may well be of value in the intellectually informative sense, but the rough-and-tumble attempts of the study and discussion group to determine relevance presents the present as the center ring for significant attention. As David Hunter has urged: " If God is really to be found by any of us, he is to be found in the present, not in the past. He was known in the past, and we can know about him in the past, as we must, but we can only encounter him and know ourselves in the present." [28]

Thus all these and other resources not mentioned herein provide the Christian educator with significant opportunities and means to present both the course and the content of the Christian faith to those whose appetites are indicated by their presence. Each and all of these offer the individual a chance to interpolate in terms of his or her own life experiences, to share with and learn from others whose experiences have been perhaps similar, perhaps dissimilar. Perhaps most important, they offer the opportunity for encounter, to wrestle spiritually, intellectually, and emotionally with the problems and questions of interpretation and application of the fullness of God's providential gifts as they are perceived.

Without such opportunity, the conversion of the individual is no deep-down conversion, and the resultant commitment is not sufficiently grounded to withstand the stress and strain of the changes and chances of mortal life. " The meaning of the faith does not become clear until one has made his personal decision, and has begun to participate in the reality of the story of sin and grace as his own story." [29]

## *Chapter Eight*

# THE FACES OF RESISTANCE

The resources enumerated in the previous chapter are but a few of the more apparent of a great number. Many such resources are not recognized because of their unfamiliarity, but a number of them are not taken into account simply because they are taken for granted. There is virtually no experience or emotion that does not contribute either positively or negatively to the awareness and development of selfhood. The resources for the attainment of Christian selfhood, however, do not exist in a kind of blessed vacuum, waiting like a mother lode to be tapped and utilized. The resources for self-realization and self-fulfillment are not in isolation but in relation to all of life, components of the dynamic flux of events and influences, and sometimes the relationship is one of conflict rather than support. As there are many traditions and truths that contribute to the attainment of selfhood in the Judeo-Christian pattern, so are there many tensions and trials that stand in opposition. The historical paradox of the Christian church is that it has always been strongest during its periods of persecution. It is, therefore, not only necessary but perhaps beneficial to recognize and acknowledge the various factors and faces of resistance to the developing consciousness and consummation of the self.

Basically, there are only two faces of resistance. The term " face " is used because each face has the possibility and the practice of many expressions, and because each represents a larger whole, an attitude or spirit, that permeates and activates a body of people. The term is also applicable because a face may often give the appearance of something in which the body does not have genuine credence. Thus in the case of the following two faces of resistance, the outward and visible sign must not be accepted as definitive, for the appearances may be both false and deceptive. Resistance there may be, and it seems to be strong, but it may not be sincerely felt. On the contrary, the token of acceptance must not be permitted to disguise the reality of resistance where it exists.

The first face of resistance is that of the culture itself, perhaps the most difficult of definition and proscription. If the Christian faith is suprahistorical, it is certainly supracultural and supranational. In that sense, Christianity may be said to be a destructive force, for it breaks down or transcends the walls of partition where and as they exist, in the interest and the name of the unity of the sons of God. Where it fails in this task or is compromised in the accomplishment of it, the eternal and comprehensive faith is weakened and its saving relevance is qualified.

Any attempt to distinguish between the resistance of the culture to the communication of Christian understanding and the achievement of the self-integrity that is the birthright of all men must of necessity be concerned with the manifestations of that resistance. The ethos of resistance is not universal and is not subject to any generalized definition, but only to specific recognition and delineation. At the risk of defining symptom rather than disease, but with a view toward sensing the condition of the whole from an examination of some of its parts, certain characteristics of contemporary culture present themselves for scrutiny as those aspects of life which the individual in search of selfhood encounters as resistance.

The first of these is not peculiar to contemporary culture. Every culture has been and is, to some extent, provincial, localized, unwilling to accept its place as but a portion of eternity. The occasions it celebrates are too often attributed to itself and its genius alone, whereas the evidences of its fail-

ures and inadequacies are laid at the door of its predecessors. It is, of course, a truism to say that no culture is independent of those with whom it lives and those from whom it came. At least to some degree, every culture is related to its contemporaries and is derivative of its forebears. Thus the occasions for pride as well as those for panic are not distinct and unrelated. They are recognizable elements in the continuum, the total fabric of history. Thus an unreasonable and unrealistic isolationism is the first mark of cultural resistance to anything that testifies to something beyond its temporally oriented existence.

Secondly, contemporary culture experiences the results of its rapid technological advance as a mixture of bane and blessing. " Man in the nuclear age is painfully, agonizingly aware that something is wrong with him. He is nervous. He is afraid. On the one hand he is the slave to schedule, on the other, he is bored and lonely in his leisure." [1] Of the various peculiarities that mark our contemporary culture, technology is certainly entitled to a place of high priority. The age of the atom has resulted in the age of automation, and this is experienced in everything from " the burner with a brain " in the kitchen to the complicated control mechanisms of spacecraft. When the decisions of a computer are proved to be more rational and more dependable than those of its inventors, have we any right to expect less than resistance to that which defines the individual as a subject of ultimate worth?

Both cultural isolationism and technological exploits contribute to a third form of cultural resistance, which manifests itself in a secular and humanistically based vanity. This is experienced by the individual in search of his selfhood as a general unease of the spirit which refuses to accept the seeming truth of temporal limitation and resists the shallow assurance of a transient security. In a virtual " textbook illustration " of the mechanism of defense, contemporary culture feeds its ego by resisting and resenting that which speaks of a suprahistorical orientation. It seeks doggedly and sometimes with a too obvious desperateness to rationalize and jus

tify its significance apart from any ground or fulfillment not of its own creation or desire. The tension of this conflict is reflected in the life and work of the individual and is especially apparent in these days as we stand poised in the gateway to outer space. The creativity of the culture has outdistanced both its comprehension and possibly its control.

The heart of the problem is that the earth dwellers, whether they live in eastern or western hemispheres, have not prepared themselves adequately for the journey into space. We have directed our attention to machinery rather than motives. We have been concerned with blast-off when we should have been thinking about basic purposes. In a more general sense our education bears all the marks of specific earth gravity. We have been part of the cosmos but we have tended to regard it as scenery rather than a total abode. Copernicus, Einstein, and Shapley notwithstanding, man still sees man as the center of the universe. We have cheapened our Gods by cutting them down to accessible size and separating them from a concept beyond infinity. It is as though we had been preparing for Beethoven by listening to hyenas.[2]

The rapidity with which man's horizons have expanded, particularly in the last half century, the extent of his researches and resourcefulness, the wide scope of his activities and events, have all contributed to the cultural credo that ours is certainly the greatest if not the best of all possible worlds. And by the doorway of this delusion we enter the realm of the fourth manifestation of cultural resistance to that which has its origin and its destiny beyond this world. The discoveries that have revealed unsuspected dimensions in both the physical and the psychical realms have made adjustment to astounding revelations almost a matter of course. From the most bestial of murders to the most thrilling of medical discoveries, the reaction is all too often the same nod of the head or monosyllabic acknowledgment that greets a reminder to put gasoline in the car! This symptom of the face of cultural resistance is the one of desensitization or insensitivity.

Here, too, we have a resultant of cultural isolationism. It

is one of some importance for the individual who seeks to comprehend the significance of a selfhood neither created nor limited by a so-powerful society. Unquestionably there is conflict here, and the issue is joined within the individual, for he is the microcosm of the culture even as the culture is the macrocosm of the individuals who comprise it. When the struggle becomes too intense, too painful, the easy avenue of escape is that of abdication. Like Scarlett O'Hara, who promised to " think about that tomorrow," many a modern individual postpones his feeling until a vague and distant " tomorrow."

It has been said that one of the greatest crimes against life is not to feel. " And there was never, perhaps, a civilization in which that crime, the crime of torpor, of lethargy, of apathy, the snake-like sin of coldness-at-the-heart was commoner than in our technological civilization in which the emotionless emotions of adolescent boys are mass produced on television screens to do our feeling for us, and a woman's longing for her life is twisted, by singing commercials, into a longing for a new detergent, family size, which will keep her hands as innocent as though she had never lived." [3]

One result of this tendency to desensitization, this unwillingness to accept reality for and as it is, is the practice of specious concern for substitutes and superficialities. More importantly, however, it precludes the possibility of solution, for cure is dependent upon correct diagnosis. A broken limb has never been correctly set by the application of Merthiolate to a pimple on the nose! Recognition does not necessarily result in resolution, but difficulties and disagreements must be correctly defined if there is to be any possibility of accurate solution. Furthermore, the avoidance of reality involves not merely indulgent disregard of evils but, more unfortunately, the failure to recognize and accept the inspiration of live possibilities and actual accomplishments.

An age which is desensitized to evils and horrors is also desensitized to its glories and its opportunities. The essential task, then, is to regenerate the vital responses, to reopen access to the clarifying functions of conscience, to restore the capacity to dream about a better life. Despite all the billowing evidence to the contrary, man is still capable of good purposes and decent works. He can still recapture command of his existence and the forces that are shaping it. And this regeneration requires only an experience in self-recognition to be real.[4]

A fifth demonstration of cultural resistance to that which comes from beyond itself is found in the individual and corporate evidences of irresponsibility for the welfare and well-being of others. This is most obvious in the rapid increase of crime. Contrary to much uninformed opinion, this increase is not restricted to the juvenile age group. The present adolescent society may not be either the best or the worst the world has ever known, but it is certainly the most publicized! It is well to remember that the so-called juvenile delinquent is living with youthful zest and ambition in the image of the adult delinquent who spawned him. Our children live not so much in isolation as they live in imitation, and for every juvenile form of addiction, there will be found an adult counterpart. At every age level, the increasing violations of the rights, privileges, possessions, and even personalities of others is but a logical consequence of a moral relativism whose fires are fed by the fuel of a hedonistic immediacy.

Where there is no accepted standard of moral values upheld and practiced by the free consent of the majority, there will, of necessity, be selfish actions irrelevantly justified on the basis of subjective interpretations or palmed off just as irrelevantly as the result of external environmental factors. When man is cut adrift from the ground, the purpose, and the hope of his being, the law of the jungle and a misconstruction of the Darwinian hypothesis takes over. The road to destruction may be long and deceptive of its end, but for those who have eyes to see and ears to hear, the warnings are apparent and the destination clearly to be perceived.

Our society has become so bad and so criminal only because she has respected nothing but her own preservation or a good reputation in history. Society has indeed lost all contact with the sacred. But society began in the nineteenth century to find a substitute for religion by proposing herself as an object of adoration. The doctrines of evolution and the notions of selection that accompany them have made of the future of society a final end. The political utopias that were grafted onto those doctrines placed at the end of time a golden age that justified in advance any enterprises whatever.[5]

In perhaps no other area is the truth of the above indicated more clearly than the adolescent exuberance of the American political system, the sixth symptom of cultural resistance. There is a colloquialism to the effect that you cannot argue with success, and on this petard the critics of " the American way " have been frequently and joyously hoisted. It is true that the appetite for this sport has abated somewhat since the McCarthy experience, but there are still those who insist that criticism or even expression of concern is tantamount to disloyalty and should be dealt with as such.

At the risk of such censure, however, certain facts are apparent. These facts challenge the Christian in the local community as he attempts to reconcile the conduct and the core of his life with the redemptive working of God in history. Despite the touting of democracy, resistance to the development of the self is experienced wherever the caste system is found in social and vocational life. The freedom of the people is so highly prized or the fear of the free exercise of their franchise is so great that only one half to three fourths of the registered population vote in local, state, and national elections. The elected representatives of the people feel their provincial responsibilities so keenly that major depressed areas are ignored in favor of that grand American political tradition, " the pork-barrel bill." The disregard for both public and private rights of minority groups is brought to attention only as prelude and postlude to election campaigns and, in the interim, are conveniently considered for " study " or " survey."

The face of our resistance in this instance is deceiving, for we are, except when caught or crossed, as Frank Gibney has defined us, " A Genial Society." The truth of the matter is that we are far removed from the " watchful beginnings in the midst of what the Puritans (before they started to make money) liked to call ' this evil, sinful world.' The Genial Society takes abundance for granted. Its members are paradoxically careless of the possessions they seek so avidly, once they get them — they are so used to planned obsolescence. Yet while lacking the vigilance of the miser, they retain all of the miser's acquisitiveness." [6] Thus we see the result of a political philosophy that, guided by a vague deism and a vigorous rationalism, perverted the religious concept of a promised land to an easy and irresponsible acceptance of a " deserved " land.

As a philosophy, Western democratic capitalism may be most conducive to the care and concern of the individual. But this is not to say it is an adequate or appropriate substitute for the purpose and love of God for his children. All provincialism, all nationalism, falls short of the inheritance prepared for the sons of God by the creator of heaven and earth. The Christian is compelled to recognize both sides of the coin, as in the Biblical injunction, and even in a democracy, in the integrity of his selfhood he may have to choose for God rather than an elected Caesar.

The resistance to the development of selfhood offered by contemporary political philosophy, even one as well-intentioned as American democracy, is perhaps most clearly seen in the continuing struggle against the politicoeconomic growth of communism. The Christian has a difficult time indeed if he dares to assert that neither democracy nor communism may be the full flowering of the Kingdom of God in history. Should he be so bold in this land of the free as to assert that communism may be an instrument of God, raised by him to chastise a complacent and compromising society even as centuries ago he raised Chaldea to smite Israel, the contemporary individual may find himself in straits similar to those experienced by Isaiah and Jeremiah when they questioned the validity of the race for power and the confidence in armed and political might.

The " American way " may or may not be the Christian way, and the worship of democracy and the government of " free " men may be as idolatrous as the worship of the golden calf. The present fear of communism, of course, renders such expressions highly suspect and, indeed, dangerous. Thus the prevailing political philosophy, supposedly a derivative of Christian understanding, may be a source of resistance to both Christian work and witness and the ideals of the political systems under which we live in this world.

Prof. G. T. Robinson, while head of the Russian Institute at Columbia University, cautioned us about this very thing by reminding us that in our concern over what communism may do to democracy we have tended to overlook the danger of what we ourselves may do to democracy under the stimulus of fear. Fighting fire with fire is an easy but misleading slogan that has betrayed more than one cause. Challenged by authoritarianism, men begin to build an authoritarianism of their own; they tend to take on the mood and techniques of their opponents; they answer heresy-hunting with heresy-hunting; they become like the thing they fight. If the Soviet tactics have succeeded in inducing us to measure loyalty by conformity, they have maneuvered us into retreating from the field before the battle has even begun. This is what fear can do to people.[7]

The second face of resistance encountered by the individual in search of self-understanding and self-fulfillment, exists, paradoxically, on the very ground where persons might expect to find their greatest support for search and encouragement for successful accomplishment — the contemporary church. Under the guise of humility, the church has allowed itself to be humiliated, to be used as an instrument of cultural convenience. Like the best china, it is brought out from its safe place to bless everything from sales conventions to professional football games, and the invocations on such occasions are matched in irrelevance only by their length! The church functions significantly in the contemporary culture as a real estate broker, renting appropriate spaces for baptisms, marriages, and funerals. Small wonder that many in our time, seeking a way not so much to escape as to encounter, climb a figurative tree so that like Zacchaeus of old, they may have a clearer view of the reality of incarnate love and action.

The contemporary church qualifies as a face and a force of resistance rather than a resource for the development of selfhood because in startling measure it has turned from the worship of the reconciling Christ to the wisdom and wit of the culture. The individual in search of his saving Lord is hard pressed to find any who have heard his voice or felt the touch of his hand. Confused by the urbane preachments of an aesthetically sophisticated clergy, he patiently requests like the New Testament Greeks to "see Jesus." As L. Nelson Bell has recognized, "We live in a time when culture and social graces are confused with Christianity; when a 'decent life' precludes the necessity of facing up to our own sinfulness; in a time when the average church member seems to feel that in some measure he is doing God a favor by engaging in church activities." [8]

The desire of the individual to discover and develop his selfhood under God, with the help of the resources native to Christian nurture, encounters resistance in the form of the organized church, which places more importance on agreement with the culture than acknowledgment of the pastoral responsibility. The resistance to the tentative religious response is not so much overt as it is, more often, demonstrated by an inertia, a reluctance to depart from the tried and accepted — in the sense of successful rather than faithful — methods of communication. This is evidenced by news releases which speak more of vanity than of vision, by a concern for status and statistics rather than simplicity and sincerity, by an emphasis on physical plant, number of members, and outward growth rather than educational program, conversion experiences, and inward depth. In far too many of the contemporary Christian centers, the token tithe replaces constant and consistent witness to a truth not of our own devising as the definitive element. There is always the convenient envelope for the casual attender, and far more time is spent reminding the members of unpaid pledges than in remonstrating with them for failures in the faith.

Another aspect of the resistance of the contemporary church is to be noted by a study of its written and verbal communications as contrasted with those of the church of the first three centuries. Naturally, this has a disturbing and disruptive influence on the sincere search for selfhood. Personal confrontation with the risen Christ represented by his body, the church, has given way to a program carried on with the cultural seal of approval, bestowed primarily for a high degree of innocuousness. The individual who seeks a deeper and more meaningful level of community nourishment is often frustrated and failed by the current concern and practice, especially in what are termed "the established churches." Into such a "successful" local church must come the repentant realization that "Christianity is not what a group of contemporary Christians want to make it as a result of their own experience. It is the response within contemporary experience to what is given in the historical revelation." [9]

This depth of understanding and conversion is particularly difficult to attain in the American churches because the materialism of our society and the secularism of our national philosophy is shot through the "religious" life of the nation. A recent editorial in *Christianity Today* pointed this out and suggested that "the Church, once the center of our American way of life, has become, in many instances, a matter of temples where we gather for an hour a week to hear something good about a good life." [10] The significance of this is especially evident in the religious illiteracy of our children. Not only are they significantly ill-informed, but such information as is imparted to them is irrelevant either to the historic teaching of the church or to the decisions that they are daily called upon to make in the process of living a life at any age. One critic of the modern scene summed it up by saying, "Our children see and hear too much about the almighty dollar and too little about Almighty God, too much about pleasure and too little about values, too much about fashions and too little about manners." [11]

It may appear paradoxical to define as a face of resistance one supposedly prime area of resource, but the semblance of the church is not to be confused with its actuality. In many areas, the contemporary Christian community has taken on more of the credoes of the culture than the creeds of its faith or the cross of its Lord. H. S. Elliott reminds us that the local churches "are very human societies, dominated to a large degree by the practice and standards of the society of which they are a part. Church members, accustomed to life on a competitive basis, bring into their church relationships the attitudes and techniques they have developed in other aspects of life — the rivalries and jealousies, the efforts to win at the expense of others, the tendencies to seek personal reward and recognition." [12]

Although the church is the place to which such ideas should be brought in repentance and for sanctification, the concern for the codes and customs of the culture gives to them a greater credence than they deserve and demonstrates an insecurity and uncertainty with regard to the principles and practices of the Christian faith insufficient to redeem them. The seeking individual, needing reassurance along the way of his pilgrimage, does not find it in the vacillations and accommodations of the local Christian group oriented as it is more to the desires and demands of the secular community than to the challenge and charge of its Christ, the sure foundation on which he can take his stand with either confidence or conviction. It is little wonder that his attempts to believe are at first seemingly reinforced but eventually overcome by what appears to be proof positive, yet results in a superficial quality of membership in a society that blithely and blasphemously guarantees success in this world and salvation in the next.

One of the sharpest critics of "the culture church" is

Martin Marty, who is further distinguished by the fact that he offers not merely criticism and penetrating analysis, but is bold enough to suggest possibilities for resolution and reconstruction.

The problem of religionized America was this: everyone was "religious" and so it was hard for anyone to be religious. That is, when a culture-religion sank root in our society, taking captive with it much of the impulse of Biblical religion, it became difficult to see the need for deeper commitment and larger service. Culture-religion is by its nature all-inclusive; it offers without demanding and satiates without inspiring. Against this background the Christian parish, if it is to have something to say to society and if it is to represent him who "came to seek and to save that which was lost," must somehow begin its work by expressing a sense of "the Difference." [13]

This area of "the Difference" is where the individual in search of his selfhood experiences primarily the resistance of the culture-oriented church. For it is when the individual feels himself "called in" to the world to "call out" against those forces and philosophies that would deter him from or deny him his birthright that he separates himself from the crowd and challenges the laissez-faire witness of "cultured" Christianity. It is not only paradoxical but tragic that where the secular world expects the Christian to cry out in condemnation and for correction, the religious organization tends to restrain him from this witness and to remonstrate with him for choosing — by its standards — a less excellent way. The world may not be waiting for the sunrise, but increasingly there is evidence that it awaits the sincerity in practice of the vocation that is professed.

What the world expects of Christians is that Christians should speak out, loud and clear, and that they should voice their condemnation in such a way that never a doubt, never the slightest doubt, could rise in the heart of the simplest man. That they should get away from abstraction and confront the blood-stained face history has taken on today. The grouping we need is a grouping of men resolved to speak out clearly and to pay up personally.[14]

The plea for reality and actuality comes from both outside and inside the church as we know it today. The recognition of it and response to it is vital if the church is to fulfill its function as a community and minister to the individual as he attempts to comprehend and respond to the prior claim of God upon his life. Confronted as we are by contemporary evidence, one is reminded of the saying that one can take care of one's enemies, but requires deliverance from one's friends. Toleration is a word that in its poorest meaning is foreign to the Christian commission, and yet we find the contemporary church tolerating many things that are inimical to its purpose and contrary to its profession in the interest of the continuing acceptance by the culture. It may well be made clear when the final curtain is lowered on the drama of God's action in history that the apparent enemy was the greatest friend.

Ever since the time of Constantine it has been evident that not persecution but cultural acceptance has been the most insidious enemy of faithful Christian practice. Fundamentally, the church is commissioned in the pattern of its Lord "to be so uniquely and aggressively different that it will have a redemptive influence upon every aspect of society." [15] When it fails to do or be this, seeking instead the approbation of a less-informed and secular authority, it betrays its trust and denies its potential for the individual. It serves instead only as a force of resistance rather than a resource to the development of responsible selfhood, endeavoring to learn of and respond to that which is not bound by immediate space and present time.

To overcome this resistance, there is a need for reform. At the heart of such a reform movement, however, there must be an illuminated and inspired concern for the individual and a firm and faithful intent to minister to the searching self in such a way that it will be an aid to discovery rather than a barrier to realization. Instead of identifying with the culture, the church needs to distinguish itself from it. It must, in the name of God, be more concerned for its nurturing responsibility than for its current rating in the popularity poll. To be all things to all men is an admirable effort, but the concern for breadth and scope must not disallow or disregard the need for depth. From behind the sanctity of its Gothic or the striking appearance of its A-frames, the church must come into the real world of action and accident, observing and listening to its people and sharing with them in the conquests and the chaos.

The church needs to establish new standards of evaluation which are not borrowed from the secular culture. The focus of this measurement must be what is actually happening to participants, rather than merely counting them. It is entirely appropriate to seek to serve ever greater numbers of people. But the church errs when it assumes that doing this is primary evidence of effective religious nurture.[16]

The individual who faces the contemporary church, seeking for the truth it holds in sacred trust and encountering, instead, resistance to his search, experiences a tension within himself that is comparable to the tension which exists in principle between the church and the world. All too often the Christian standard of life is replaced by the American standard of living. The word of God to the prophet, " Comfort ye, comfort ye my people," is perverted to justify a ministry of comforting the comfortable. The community of commitment established by the renunciation and dedication of Holy Baptism is exchanged for a society of the culturally qualified. The church dons its face of resistance when it fails the individual in his need and his aspiration by proclaiming an ethic of love and practicing an ethic of ease, by professing a discipleship of the Lord Christ and promoting a fellowship of " fun."

These, then, are the two prime faces of resistance, each of which has many expressions. They provide the prime barriers to self-understanding and self-fulfillment. They are in not-so-loyal opposition to the resources that are available to the individual for the development of his selfhood. Christian concern for the self, however, will make such use of the resources of both this world and the next that such resistance will be recognized and redeemed, for the confidence of the Christian is that so clearly expressed by Martin Luther:

> Did we in our own strength confide,
>   Our striving would be losing;
> Were not the right Man on our side,
>   The Man of God's own choosing:
> Dost ask who that may be?
>   Christ Jesus, it is he;
> Lord Sabaoth his name,
>   From age to age the same,
> And he must win the battle.

## *Chapter Nine*

# THE HOPE OF RESOLUTION

That educational and pastoral concern of the Christian church reflected most clearly in the nurturing role is directed specifically and most significantly toward the individual. With God at the center of its being and purpose, Christian education and Christian pastoral care strive to be so cognizant of and concerned for the individual that he may be brought " into the right relationship with God and his fellows within the perspective of the fundamental Christian truths about all of life." [1]

A study of the history of Christian education as a formal endeavor reveals a series of alternate emphases. During one period the greatest burden of concern is for the communication of the centrality of God. During another period the greater stress is placed upon the needs of man. The truth of the matter is that Christian education can never be concerned with either one to the exclusion of the other. Equal attention must be paid to both and, more importantly, to the relationship between them, for therein lies the dynamic. As L. J. Sherrill has maintained, the proper orientation of Christian education is bipolar: " It is concerned with the *meeting* between God and the human creature, and with the tension which rises within the encounter, calling for human response to God and for divine response to man." [2]

Effective nurturing activity by the Christian church can never be directed toward a group or class. To the degree to which it is true to its function and responsible to its purpose, Christian education must always be directed solely to and for the individual. The concern of Christian education must always be for persons, not generically but specifically. The social or communal nature of the task must never take priority over the individual, for the former derives its strength and meaning only from the latter.

This dual aspect of the nurturing task in the Christian community, but with the priority of concern for the individual, emphasizes the element of confrontation that precedes conversion and commitment. Paul Vieth asserts that the process is both individual and social by virtue of the uniqueness of each person and the deeply corporate sense of true Christian community. By such a relationship the past informs the present and thereby cultivates and illuminates a valid estimate of the future. Such a view also provides a necessary breadth of scope for acceptance of the individual and acknowledgment of his need for community.[3]

Stephen Neill points out that generalizations can be made only if their "approximative" character is recognized, for "the individual has a habit, infuriating to the systematic and orderly mind, of escaping from the generalisations under which it is supposed that he had been subsumed."[4] Thus the so-called laws of human nature do not apply restrictively to Christian education. In the service of its Lord, Christian education must reflect his sensitivity to and awareness of individual variations, both positive and negative. As his chosen instrument of communication, Christian education must speak *personally* to every man, woman, and child as he spoke, with sympathetic awareness of peculiar conditions and relevant counsel for understanding and growth.

The nurturing activity of the Christian church is concerned to present so relevantly the truth of God in Christ to the individual that he will respond and, in the responding, become aware and accepting of his selfhood. The nurturing task is to present the individual not so much with a pattern as with a purpose, not so much with a demand as with a desire.

The community from which the individual is alienated is the very one in which the fullness of his selfhood can be acknowledged and appreciated. In this nurturing activity, therefore, the church must be willing to see the individual as he sees himself. It must, in fact, help him to see himself, to recognize the depth of his despair and, *on that level,* the relevance of the redemptive opportunity that is his.

No matter how unpleasant such recognition may be, no matter how comforting a false sense of cultural security may feel, to disavow the seriousness of the separation, to ignore the fact of the individual's sin of separation, is, in the final analysis, a denial of his existential individuality and a disregard for the integrity of the self and the responsibility of the pastoral charge. Any superficial acceptance is not educative in the redemptive sense of the term. It is, rather, destructive, for it disdains the individual's knowledge of himself and thereby endangers the very foundations of selfhood. " Integrity of the self is the main source of strength in the individual. To be untrue to oneself, dishonest or insincere may result in self-impairment." [5] The group or society that permits — let alone fosters — this kind of superficiality by its acceptance of only the acceptable, stands in the way of selfhood instead of contributing to its development and accomplishment.

It would appear, therefore, that there is a need for the individual to be not only permitted but encouraged to recognize himself, the height and depth and breadth of what he knows himself to be. It is only by the understanding we call self-understanding that the need and relevance of the reconciling love of God can become clear. Unless and until the fullness of the need as well as the extent of the separation is comprehended by the individual and realized by the community, the redemptive truth that is the core of the Christian action will not penetrate the walls of the cultural prison. The essence of this activity, this ministry, is particularity of personality.

Carl Jung has noted that the individual is characterized by the unique, not the regular, by the singular, not the universal. "There is and can be no self-knowledge based on theoretical assumptions, for the object of self-knowledge is an individual — a relative exception and an irregular phenomenon." [6]

The prime difference between the Christian community and other forms of community is not so much in its desire for strength as in its willingness to accept weakness, and in its ability, by the indwelling power of the Holy Spirit, to transform that weakness into strength. This is to the benefit of both the individual and the Christian community. The individual is accepted into the Christian community, not despite his limitations, but with a full acceptance of these as a natural consequence of his human existence. This acceptance by the Christian community is a verification of his own self-understanding, which is based on a realistic appraisal and acknowledgment of both strengths and weaknesses.

The beginning of growth is when a person accepts his limitations, and realizes that he is acceptable in spite of his inferiorities. These inferiorities then become his bond of unity with the rest of humankind, not badges of his isolation from others. They become, not blind driving forces that compel him unconsciously to present a superiority façade that accentuates other people's difference from and inferiority to him. Rather, his inferiorities become marks of the dying of an old self and the birth of a new life of inner security. These inferiorities are no longer the tortuous treadmill of one feverish act of meritorious appeal for approval after another until one faints from exhaustion. These marks of inferiority become transformed into altars of acceptance by *grace,* unearned, unmerited, unsought for – gifts of the Spirit of God.[7]

The conduct of this growth, as well as the opportunity for it, are marks of the freedom that is the birthright of the individual. This freedom "consists of the movement of the person toward the discovery of his own inner integrity and capacity for self-direction." [8] When man understands that he is free to act, free to choose in terms of his needs as he understands them, he tends to respond with an equal measure of responsibility. Usually he does not violate the trust that has been expressed and in such a context " individual integrity is maintained and fostered and society is enriched." [9]

The nurturing activity of the Christian church is concerned for the communication of the availability to mankind of this gift of freedom. In effect, " the whole ministry of the Church is the effort to communicate the freedom of God." [10] Thus the church penetrates the loneliness of separated man and speaks clearly of his place and priority in the order of creation. It holds out to the individual the privilege of accepting that high place and, by his acceptance, effecting the necessary reconciliation between himself and God and himself and his fellowman.

> The inestimable gift of the gospel is our freedom to become what we *are* already in the eyes of God. Man's freedom is the expression of his uniqueness, his integrity and self-awareness, his capacity to act and to decide for himself, his imaginative participation in more than one realm of time and space, his response and his gift-giving in love. This is freedom. It is more than a mere capacity for choice. It is the fulfillment of the gift which God made possible when he laid the foundation of the earth and set man in the midst of it.[11]

Christian education is charged with the communication of the truth of God in relation to the needs of man. The Messianic injunction to " go and teach " is a specific implementation of the pastoral directive to " feed my sheep." Christian education must be open to both God and man in such a way and in order that through its clear channel each may pass to the other. The nature of God and his involvement in the human situation is vital to the proper exercise and understanding of the nurturing function of Christian education. The concern of this aspect of the church's life must be not only for content but for the means and methods of communication, for truth is communicated by the very means or methodology selected for its communication.[12]

If it is true that personality is dynamic and not static, and that it is communicated primarily through experience, through relationship, rather than by the consideration of impersonal content, then the reality of God as Person is not communicated so much through the presentation of intellectual affirmation and argument as it is through response to revelation. The intensely personal nature of such an encounter brings the realization that God is indeed a Person and at work in this world in the individual lives of his children whether they know it or not, and in spite of the fact that they may choose to deny or reject it. "God is personal and self-conscious, intelligent and purposeful, good and just and loving, and capable of communication and communion with human persons. He has none of the limitations of human personality, and yet he has all the qualities which make him supremely personal." [13]

The vitality of the relationship between the self and God intrudes upon and illuminates all the areas of human effort and aspiration. The wonder of God's involvement in individuality is the starting point for the comprehension of the fullness of his love. One relates to God as Person, not as force or plan. Thus it is an experience of encounter rather than collision. It is not so much a matter of intellectual apprehension as it is a relationship of personal commitment.

> The self is not related to God by sharing its reason with God and finding a point of identity with the divine through the rational faculty. The self is related to God in repentance, faith and commitment. All these forms of relation imply a certain degree of existential discontinuity with God. The self is always a creature, conscious of its finiteness, and equally conscious of its pretension in not admitting its finiteness. Insofar as it becomes conscious of its pretensions it is capable of repentance and a new life. The encounter with God is in short a dramatic one.[14]

The positive results of this encounter are seen in the resultant freedom with which the self operates in this world which has previously been experienced as a threat to selfhood. The full sense of life is gained from the relationship to and with God. The courage for living is derived from the assurance of the abiding presence of God. The purpose of life is visualized out of the comfort of the abiding love of God. Thus there comes, from this relationship, the development and utilization, on man's part, of the fullness of selfhood for which he was created and intended. The positive evidences are portrayed with compelling clarity in the following analysis:

> The person who has become a self before God can give himself with an abandon that has been purged of hesitation and division of spirit. He can genuinely be anxious for nothing – that is, have no need for idolatrous defenses, no need for hesitation, and no need for fretful preoccupation of the spirit. He can cast all these cares upon God, for God is his defense, his purpose, and the inhabitant of his inner being.[15]

This is the goal of man's searching activity. It is the reward of his effort to synthesize the reality of his existence with the revelation of his purpose. It is the victory that results from the overcoming of temporal resistance by the power of eternal resource, the welcome end to the significant journey that we have called " The Return to Self-Concern."

# NOTES

*INTRODUCTION*

1. Erich Fromm, "Selfishness, Self-Love, and Self-Interest," in C. E. Moustakas, ed., *The Self: Explorations in Personal Growth* (Harper & Brothers, 1956), p. 67.
2. C. E. Moustakas, "True Experience and the Self," in Moustakas, *op. cit.,* p. 8.
3. David Granskou, "The Concept of Selfhood in the New Testament and Modern Ethics," *Religion in Life,* Vol. XXX, No. 1 (Winter, 1960–1961), pp. 92–93.
4. Gordon W. Allport, *The Individual and His Religion* (The Macmillan Company, 1959), p. 70.
5. Charles R. Stinnette, Jr., *Faith, Freedom, and Selfhood* (The Seabury Press, Inc., 1959), p. 83.
6. Paul H. Vieth, ed., *The Church and Christian Education* (published for the Cooperative Publishing Association by The Bethany Press, 1947), p. 44.
7. Carl G. Jung, *The Undiscovered Self,* trans. by R. F. C. Hall (Little, Brown and Company, 1958), p. 111.
8. Jung, *op. cit.,* pp. 41–42.

*CHAPTER ONE*

1. Cf. Paul Tillich, *Theology of Culture,* ed. by R. C. Kimball (Oxford University Press, Inc., 1959), Ch. 4.
2. David E. Roberts, *Psychotherapy and a Christian View of Man* (Charles Scribner's Sons, 1950), p. 31.
3. Lewis Joseph Sherrill, *The Gift of Power* (The Macmillan Company, 1955), p. 120. Used by permission.

4. Tillich, *op. cit.,* p. 43.
5. Erich Fromm, *Man for Himself* (Rinehart & Co., Inc., 1947), p. 194.
6. Jung, *op. cit.,* p. 72.
7. Tillich, *op. cit.,* p. 46.
8. Albert Camus, *Resistance, Rebellion, and Death,* trans. by Justin O'Brien (Alfred A. Knopf, 1961), pp. 253–254.
9. Doris E. Thompson, "Letters to the Editor," *The Living Church,* July 15, 1962, p. 3.
10. Elton Trueblood, *The Company of the Committed* (Harper & Brothers, 1961), p. 10.
11. Martin E. Marty, *The New Shape of American Religion* (Harper & Brothers, 1958), p. 117.
12. L. Nelson Bell, "The Joy of Salvation," *Christianity Today,* June 19, 1961, p. 17.
13. Trueblood, *op. cit.,* pp. 8–9.
14. Paul Elmen, *The Restoration of Meaning to Contemporary Life* (Doubleday & Company, Inc., 1958), pp. 59–60.
15. Erich Fromm, *Psychoanalysis and Religion* (Yale University Press, 1950), p. 118.

## *CHAPTER TWO*

1. Stephen Neill, *A Genuinely Human Existence* (Doubleday & Company, Inc., 1959), p. 73.
2. Stinnette, *op. cit.,* p. 70.
3. Vance Packard, *The Hidden Persuaders* (David McKay Company, Inc., 1957).
4. Wayne E. Oates, *Anxiety in Christian Experience* (The Westminster Press, 1955), p. 31.
5. Paul Tillich, *The Courage to Be* (Yale University Press, 1952), p. 47.
6. Stinnette, *op. cit.,* p. 85.
7. *Ibid.,* p. 6.
8. Jung, *op. cit.,* pp. 13–14.
9. Reinhold Niebuhr, *The Self and the Dramas of History* (Charles Scribner's Sons, 1955), p. 62. Used by permission of Charles Scribner's Sons and Faber & Faber, Ltd.
10. Stinnette, *op. cit.,* p. 88.
11. Allport, *op. cit.,* p. 93.

12. Jung, *op. cit.,* p. 112.
13. Niebuhr, *op. cit.,* p. 217.
14. Neill, *op. cit.,* p. 267.
15. P. Lecky, " The Personality," in Moustakas, *op. cit.,* p. 91.
16. Moustakas, " True Experience and the Self," in Moustakas, *op. cit.,* p. 11.
17. Sherrill, *op. cit.,* p. 19.
18. Stinnette, *op. cit.,* p. 111.
19. Emil Brunner, *The Christian Doctrine of Creation and Redemption,* Vol. II: *Dogmatics,* trans. by Olive Wyon (The Westminster Press, 1952), p. 66.
20. Sherrill, *op. cit.,* p. 47.
21. *Ibid.,* p. 31.
22. Niebuhr, *op. cit.,* p. 35.
23. *Ibid.,* p. 220.
24. Sherrill, *op. cit.,* p. 10.

## *CHAPTER THREE*

1. Jung, *op. cit.,* pp. 19–20.
2. Stinnette, *op. cit.,* pp. 193–194.
3. Sherrill, *op. cit.,* p. 68.
4. *Ibid.,* p. 78.
5. Reuel L. Howe, *Man's Need and God's Action* (The Seabury Press, Inc., 1953), p. 114.
6. Harrison S. Elliott, *Can Religious Education Be Christian?* (The Macmillan Company, 1941), p. 224.
7. Sherrill, *op. cit.,* pp. 83–84.
8. *Ibid.,* p. 50.
9. Vieth, *op. cit.,* p. 134.
10. Marty, *op. cit.,* p. 112.
11. Sherrill, *op. cit.,* p. 83.
12. D. Campbell Wyckoff, *The Gospel and Christian Education* (The Westminster Press, 1959), p. 13.
13. Sherrill, *op. cit.,* p. 52.
14. H. Shelton Smith, *Faith and Nurture* (Charles Scribner's Sons, 1950), p. 90.

## CHAPTER FOUR

1. William Clayton Bower, " Recent Trends in Christian Education," *Religious Education,* July–August, 1960, p. 245.

2. Neill, *op. cit.,* pp. 50–51.
3. Oates, *op. cit.,* p. 98.
4. James D. Smart, *The Teaching Ministry of the Church* (The Westminster Press, 1954), p. 157.
5. Brunner, *op. cit.,* p. 257.
6. Daniel D. Williams, *God's Grace and Man's Hope* (Harper & Brothers, 1949), p. 79.
7. Lewis J. Sherrill, *The Rise of Christian Education* (The Macmillan Company, 1954), pp. 137–139. Used by permission.
8. Iris V. Cully, *The Dynamics of Christian Education* (The Westminster Press, 1958), p. 46.
9. Sherrill, *Gift of Power,* p. 83.

## CHAPTER FIVE

1. Sherrill, *Rise of Christian Education,* p. 209.
2. Arthur D. Nock, " Early Gentile Christianity and Its Hellenistic Background," in A. E. J. Rawlinson, ed., *Essays on the Trinity and the Incarnation* (Longmans, Green & Co., Inc., 1928), p. 154.
3. Sherrill, *Rise of Christian Education,* p. 164.
4. Vieth, *op. cit.,* p. 89.
5. Sherrill, *Rise of Christian Education,* p. 164.
6. *Ibid.,* p. 129.
7. *Ibid.,* p. 142.
8. Nock, *loc. cit.,* p. 152.
9. Sherrill, *Rise of Christian Education,* pp. 180–181.
10. Fromm, *Psychoanalysis,* p. 48.
11. Cf. Sherrill, *Rise of Christian Education,* pp. 167–197; Arthur Cushman McGiffert, *A History of Christian Thought* (Charles Scribner's Sons, 1949), Vol. I, pp. 30–258; Kendig Brubaker Cully, ed., *Basic Writings in Christian Education* (The Westminster Press, 1961), pp. 17–73, 85–132.
12. Sherrill, *Rise of Christian Education,* pp. 208–209.
13. Sherrill, *Gift of Power,* p. 57.

14. Sherrill, *Rise of Christian Education,* pp. 214–215.
15. Fromm, *Psychoanalysis,* pp. 85–86.
16. Sherrill, *Rise of Christian Education,* p. 213.
17. *Ibid.,* pp. 212–213.

## *CHAPTER SIX*

1. Franklin H. Littell, " A New View of the Laity," *Religious Education,* January–February, 1961, p. 41.
2. Niebuhr, *op. cit.,* p. 112.
3. *The Christian Century,* Vol. LXXVII (October 26, 1960), p. 1235.
4. Tillich, *The Courage to Be,* p. 163.
5. Niebuhr, *op. cit.,* p. 56.
6. Littell, *loc. cit.*
7. Cf. Henry S. Lucas, *The Renaissance and the Reformation* (Harper & Brothers, 1934), for a complete description of both the events and the effects of historical developments.
8. Cf. W. P. Witcutt, *The Rise and Fall of the Individual* (The Macmillan Company, 1958), for a comprehensive view of the so-called " autonomous " man, completely secularized after the Reformation.
9. Smith, *op. cit.,* p. 43.
10. Cf. Smart, *op. cit.,* Chs. 3 and 4, and Elliott, *op. cit.,* Ch. 3.
11. Williams, *op. cit.,* p. 34.
12. T. O. Wedel, *The Pulpit Rediscovers Theology* (The Seabury Press, Inc., 1956), pp. 10–11.
13. Smith, *op. cit.,* p. 48.
14. Elliott, *op. cit.,* pp. 278–279.
15. Smith, *op. cit.,* p. 51.
16. Elliott, *op. cit.,* p. 210.
17. Niebuhr, *op. cit.,* pp. 219–220.
18. Wyckoff, *op. cit.,* pp. 54–55.
19. Smith, *op. cit.,* p. 57.
20. Tillich, *Theology of Culture,* p. 5.
21. Roberts, *op. cit.,* p. 92.

## *CHAPTER SEVEN*

1. Granskou, *loc. cit.,* p. 104.
2. Elliott, *op. cit.,* p. 11.

3. James Daane, "Eschatology and History," *Christianity Today,* September 28, 1962, p. 12.
4. Wyckoff, *op. cit.,* p. 57.
5. Randolph Crump Miller, *The Clue to Christian Education* (Charles Scribner's Sons, 1950), p. 15.
6. Elliott, *op. cit.,* p. 233.
7. Bernhard W. Anderson, *Rediscovering the Bible* (Association Press, 1957), p. 6.
8. Sherrill, *Gift of Power,* p. 95.
9. Smart, *op. cit.,* pp. 152–153.
10. G. Ernest Wright, *God Who Acts* (Studies in Biblical Theology, No. 8; SCM Press Ltd., 1952), p. 28.
11. Anderson, *op. cit.,* p. 29.
12. Niebuhr, *op. cit.,* p. 225.
13. Smart, *op. cit.,* p. 118.
14. Niebuhr, *op. cit.,* p. 71.
15. Miller, *op. cit.,* p. 17.
16. Robert H. Bonthius, *Christian Paths to Self-Acceptance* (King's Crown Press, 1948), p. 174.
17. *Ibid.,* p. 200.
18. Roberts, *op. cit.,* p. 33.
19. Bonthius, *op. cit.,* p. 203.
20. Stinnette, *op. cit.,* p. 123.
21. Miller, *op. cit.,* p. 137.
22. Howe, *op. cit.,* p. 152.
23. Cully, Iris, *op. cit.,* p. 92.
24. Miller, *op. cit.,* p. 122.
25. Allport, *op. cit.,* p. 51.
26. Richard N. Bender, "The Scholar and the Life of the Church," *Religious Education,* September–October, 1961, p. 326.
27. Trueblood, *op. cit.,* p. 21.
28. David R. Hunter, "The Theology of Christian Education," *Religious Education,* January–February, 1963, p. 10.
29. Daniel D. Williams, "The Theological Aspect of Christian Education," *Religious Education,* March–April, 1962, p. 86.

## *CHAPTER EIGHT*

1. Chalmer E. Faw, "The Bible and Modern Man," *Christianity Today,* August 3, 1962, p. 8.

2. Norman Cousins, " Put Poets Into Space," *Saturday Review,* April 29, 1961, p. 20.

3. Archibald MacLeish, " Antidotes for Twitching," *Saturday Review,* August 12, 1961, p. 24.

4. Norman Cousins, " The Age of Desensitization," *Saturday Review,* October 27, 1962, p. 24.

5. Camus, *op. cit.,* p. 226.

6. Frank Gibney, *The Operators* (Harper & Brothers, 1960), p. 11.

7. G. T. Robinson, " The Ideological Combat," *Foreign Affairs,* July, 1949, pp. 525 ff.

8. L. Nelson Bell, *loc. cit.,* p. 17.

9. John C. Bennett, " Basic Christian Convictions," in P. H. Lotz, ed., *Orientation in Religious Education* (Abingdon-Cokesbury, 1950), p. 26.

10. " Plastic Gods and Robot Men," *Christianity Today,* December 7, 1962, p. 24.

11. Joseph H. Lookstein, " The Youth as Citizen," *Religious Education,* January–February, 1961, p. 18.

12. Elliott, *op. cit.,* p. 222.

13. Marty, *op. cit.,* p. 141.

14. Camus, *op. cit.,* p. 71.

15. Vieth, *op. cit.,* p. 173.

16. Marvin J. Taylor, " Conformity and Creativity," *Religious Education,* September–October, 1960, p. 339.

## *CHAPTER NINE*

1. Miller, *op. cit.,* p. 8.

2. Sherrill, *Gift of Power,* p. 90.

3. Vieth, *op. cit.,* p. 52.

4. Neill, *op. cit.,* p. 30.

5. Moustakas, " True Experience and the Self," in Moustakas, *op. cit.,* p. 9.

6. Jung, *op. cit.,* p. 9.

7. Oates, *op. cit.,* p. 40.

8. Stinnette, *op. cit.,* p. 51.

9. Moustakas, " True Experience and the Self," in Moustakas, *op. cit.,* p. 13.

10. Stinnette, *op. cit.,* p. 152.

11. *Ibid.,* p. 13.

12. Cf. Harry A. DeWire, *The Christian as Communicator* (The Westminster Press, 1961). This is an excellent study in considerable detail of the responsibility, means, and methodologies for the communication of Christian truth in the light of human need.

13. Miller, *op. cit.*, p. 39.

14. Niebuhr, *op. cit.*, pp. 84–85.

15. Oates, *op. cit.*, p. 156.